ARKLE

'Everyone remembers Arkle,' Michael D. Higgins, President of Ireland.

'... the greatest racehorse of all time – and that's including Mill Reef and Frankel,' Ian Balding, Flat trainer to HM The Queen, and trainer of Mill Reef.

'About time we were reading about him again,' Nicky Henderson, champion NH trainer in England, five times winner of the Arkle Chase.

'Arkle was a colossus, he was out on his own and comparisons of him with Best Mate are ludicrous,' Jim Lewis, owner of Best Mate, triple winner of the Cheltenham Gold Cup.

'*The best chaser ever*', Frank Ward, sponsor of the Arkle Chase, Leopardstown.

'*Arkle was a wonder horse,*' Stan Mellor, retired champion jockey.

'*One of the greatest of our equine stars*', Paul Greeves, Executive Director
& Keeper of the General Stud Book, Weatherbys Ltd.

'*I used to idolise Arkle … it is an honour to train a horse with a few of
Arkle's characteristics,*' Henrietta Knight writing in *Best Mate: Chasing Gold*.

'*Arkle was an exceptional horse,*' T.P. Burns, winning rider of Arkle's only flat race.

'*Arkle was second only to the Pope in Ireland – nowadays he would probably be well
ahead of the Pope!*' Emma Mac Dermott, sculptress of the new Arkle
statue in Ashbourne, Co Meath.

'At no time since Arkle have I ever come across the same magnetism or seen so much commerciality spawned as there was for Arkle,' Peter McNeile, Director of Sponsorship, Cheltenham Racecourse.

'I was nick-named Arkle at school,' Kevin Coleman, manager, Bellewstown and Laytown races.

'He would have won the Aintree Grand National standing on his head,' Lord Patrick Beresford.

'I was a nipper but I knew he was something special,' Bob Champion.

'I remember Arkle jumping it [the last fence] like a wild stag,' Joe Jones, a fan.

'We can over do the superlatives but we can't overdo them for Arkle, he was absolutely exceptional,' Sir Peter O'Sullevan, 'the voice of racing.'

'He out-stepped the Duchess,' Maureen Mullins.

'Not even Arkle could have outjumped Tarka that day!' was how the author as a young rider in a point to point captioned this photo in March 1968.

ANNE HOLLAND has written numerous non-fiction books related to horses and horse-racing, including *The Grand National: The Irish At Aintree, In the Blood: Irish Racing Dynasties, Kinane: A Remarkable Racing Family* and *Winners All: Favourite Racehorses Through the Years*, all published by The O'Brien Press. She was also a successful amateur rider.

ARKLE

THE LEGEND OF 'HIMSELF'

ANNE HOLLAND

FOREWORD BY JIM DREAPER

THE O'BRIEN PRESS
DUBLIN

CONTENTS:

Author's Note

Writing about Arkle today, half a century after his heyday, has been an immensely rewarding journey, full of surprises and new stories that are pure pleasure to share here, tempered only by the knowledge that for every new anecdote, there are doubtless dozens more still 'out there' waiting to be unearthed.

The whole Arkle story is one of those rare treats where never a bad word is heard about the main protagonists; without their guidance his journey may have taken a different path and therefore I am also including the people who were around him, from the principal players to his ardent fans.

Arkle retains his fan base fifty years on, much as his contemporaries The Beatles also continue to gain new young fans no matter how much fad or fashion may have changed. Arkle was separated from the rest of his peers, reigning in a higher stratosphere, by his incredible race record against other good horses who, without Arkle would have been stars themselves. But it was more than that. There was an aura about him. That is not imagination. 'To grow in stature like Arkle' means when a horse rises above his usual self – a bit like a bride walking down the aisle, head held high. Swagger, in either case, would be wrong. It is radiance.

To see him in the flesh was one of life's honours. Those of a certain age wallow in memories, while younger fans allow themselves to be enveloped in admiration and awe. Walk into virtually any country pub or home in Ireland, and a good few in England, and it seems there is bound to be at least one picture of Arkle. In Arkle's day, it was 'JFK (John F. Kennedy), Jesus Christ (or the Pope) and 'Himself.'

I saw him twice, both times armed with my little Kodak 'Brownie' camera: at Sandown when he put up what some aficionados consider his career best in the Gallaher Gold Cup, and at home in Box Number 7 when my sister Patsy and I had been invited over to Eva Dreaper's coming out party – a never to be forgotten trip not only for that splendid occasion in the Shelbourne Hotel, but also seeing and photographing 'Himself', and for my first visit to Dublin Horse Show (and for England winning the World Cup.)

My own family's link with Arkle came through the Dreapers – Tom Dreaper was his trainer. As a family, we first got to know the Dreapers on holiday in Kerry when Jim was ten (as he doesn't like to be reminded) and the connection continued over the years with my parents, Rex and Margaret Holland and Jim's parents, Tom and Betty Dreaper becoming firm friends for the rest of their lives. During school years, both Dreaper daughters, Eva and Valerie, at school in Kent, visited our home not far away in Sussex for roast Sunday lunches and sometimes some hunting.

Eva tells me that of the hundreds of letters to 'Himself' as Arkle became universally known, many addressed simply 'Arkle, Ireland' one came from Lithuania, revealing that the Lithuanian word for horse is 'arklys'.

Freak, phenomenon, magnificent, simply the greatest – Arkle was a superstar that makes it impossible to imagine another of his like again. He carried himself – strutted –with pride and confidence, with an imperious, majestic air. He adored the adulation he received and loved to play to the gallery; he knew he was kingpin.

His jumping could be exuberant and extravagant especially in the early stages of a race, but usually he was professional and foot perfect; very occasionally he made a mistake, but only two errors – just two in his whole career of clearing more than four hundred steeplechase fences and flights of hurdles spread over six seasons of racing – are worthy of mention: the slip on landing as a young horse in his first Hennessy at Newbury, and the wholesale monumental blunder in his final Gold Cup. The first cost him his initial duel with Mill House, the second did not so much as stall him in his tracks. He had the speed to win a flat race, a two-mile chase carrying 12 stone 11lbs, and the build and stamina to carry top weight to win the Irish Grand National, giving between two and two-and-a-half stone to his rivals.

The esteem, love and admiration with which Arkle is still held remains widespread across the whole of Irish (and English) society: a revered legend in National Hunt racing, on the Flat and among the general populace from all walks of life, from 'Joe Bloggs' to the President of Ireland.

Stories also come from unlikely sources. I was sitting in the hairdressers in Mullingar one day when another customer, hearing I was writing about Arkle, said, 'Oh, my uncle in Yorkshire named his house Arkle.'

One of my privileges has been to chat with Arkle's original 'lads', now senior citizens, his work rider Paddy Woods and his groom Johnny Lumley as well as many of the jockeys who rode against him. Jim Dreaper, son of Arkle's trainer, Tom, and his two sisters Eva and Valerie, Tom Taaffe, son of Arkle's principal rider, Pat, and ninety-three-year-old Alison Baker, daughter of Arkle's breeder, Mrs Mary Baker, have all been invaluable and I am indebted to them for their assistance, and to Jim for writing the Foreword.

In December 2012 the Irish Writers' Union held a twenty-fifth birthday party in the Guinness Storehouse, Dublin, attended by the President of Ireland, Michael D. Higgins. During his 'walkabout' after his speech, I mentioned my new project.

His response was immediate: 'Everyone remembers Arkle.'

Anne Holland
2013

ACKNOWLEDGEMENTS

Writing about Arkle has truly been a labour of love, but it would not have been possible to gain such a full account with so many anecdotes about him and those around him without help from a wide range of people, to whom I am indebted and I acknowledge their contributions with grateful thanks. The people closest to 'Himself', the Dreaper children, Eva, Jim (who both painstakingly read the script) and Valerie, the breeder's daughter Alison Baker, the jockey's son Tom Taaffe, work rider Paddy Woods and stable lad Johnny Lumley have been generous with their time, and I thank them wholeheartedly, as I also do the following, and everyone who has chatted to me about 'Himself':

Adam's (auction house, Dublin)

David Adamson

Ian Balding

Ronnie Bartlett

Sean Bell

Lord Patrick Beresford

Brenda Boyne

Susan Bradburne

Graham Budd, Graham Budd
    Auctions

James Burns

TP Burns

Pat Byrne

Helen Carr, The O'Brien Press

Sally Carroll, Irish National Stud

Bob Champion

Andrew B. Chesser

Kevin Coleman, Manager Bellewstown
    and Laytown races

Lord Patrick Connolly Carew

Valerie Cooper

Seamus Donnolly

Lynsey Dreaper

Hellen Egan

Mick Foster

Paul Greeves, Executive Director &
    Keeper of the General Stud Book,
    Weatherbys Ltd

Robert Hall

Lisa Harrison

Ronald Harrison

Eddie Harty

The Hon. Mark Hely-Hutchinson

Nicky Henderson

Theresa Hodges

Michael Hourigan

Timmy Hyde

Sinead Hyland, Irish National Stud

The Irish Field

Ruth Illingworth

Joe Jones

Michael Kauntze

Pat Keogh

Peadar Kelly

Ted Kelly

Kelly's Pub, Ashbourne

Tommy Kinane

John Kirwan

Tom Lacy

Jim Lewis

Alan Lillingston

Emma Mac Dermott

Michael McCann

Mary McGrath

Peter McNeile, Commercial Manager, Cheltenham racecourse

Cyril Maguire

Noel Meade

Meath Chronicle

Stan Mellor

Christina Mercer

Maureen Mullins

Willie Mullins

Michael Murray

Michael O'Brien, The O'Brien Press

Noel O'Brien, Senior Irish handicapper

Lissa Oliver

Jonjo O'Neill

Sir Peter O'Sullevan

Nick O'Toole

Paul Palmer, Assistant Director and General Manager, Horse Registry, Director, Weatherbys

Leo Powell

Richard Pitman

Kevin Prendergast

Penny Prendergast

GSB Ltd

Niall Reilly

Will Reilly

Peter Reynolds

Willie Robinson

Mark Roper

Jane Sandars

Jim Sheridan

Aidan Shiels

Patsy Smiles

Andrew Speedy, Racetrack

Olive Taaffe

Tom Taaffe

David Tatlow

Lord Vestey

Ted Walsh

Tom Walshe

Frank Ward

Dermot Weld

Ronnie White

John Wilson

FOREWORD

BY JIM DREAPER

You may think 'Oh, another Arkle book!' Yes indeed, and be prepared to be surprised by this one. Anne Holland, herself a very accomplished and knowledgeable horsewoman, has discovered so many stories and opinions about Arkle that even I had not known. For instance, that there had been a previous Arkle in the ownership of the Westminster family all of sixty years before THE Arkle was born. Interestingly the first Arkle was almost useless. The other one wasn't, as we know.

In spite of my family connection with Arkle and with most of the main players in his career, I am left wondering 'How had I not known this or heard that?' Anne has produced a book of so many truly interesting quotes and facts which mean a great deal to me having known the places and faces involved, all of which are part of the legend surrounding Arkle.

Anne's understanding of horses enables her to describe the good days and the not-so-good days with equal clarity, such as the puzzling work days when Arkle was unable to keep up with Flyingbolt, his younger stable mate, in a gallop on a neighbour's farm. In those days, before all-weather gallops, my father was allowed by local farmers to use many suitable fields to work the horses. However, in this case, after much wondering and head-scratching it was decided that Arkle simply did not work well in that particular field because on the few occasions that he and Flyingbolt worked there again, after that initial surprising day, the result was always the same. Flyingbolt was better there, but in light of what he was able to do on the racecourse, he may simply have been putting Arkle to the test. Many owners and trainers have had similar experiences trying to work out why horses performed differently at home than they did in race situations. They are horses, not machines – it happens.

Whatever you may know of the Arkle story, whether a little or a lot, I feel you will enjoy this account of the life and times of one of the all-time greats.

CHAPTER 1

'HE DOESN'T LOOK LIKE A RACEHORSE'

I t was the Duchess's first visit to see her new horse at Greenogue in County Meath and the yard was even more spotless than usual. The lads were well turned out and ready, holding polished headcollars; they were waiting in the feed room on the corner of the stable block, closest to the house.

Greenogue was a happy stable, but a serious one: church on Sundays and no swearing within earshot of Tom and Betty Dreaper any time. 'The weather will be just as bad without you swearing about it,' trainer Tom Dreaper would admonish. Good manners and deference were the norm in such establishments in the early 1960s.

The lads, wondering how much longer they would be waiting for Her Grace to arrive, set one of their number, one Clem Spratt, to spy through the keyhole.

'They're coming!' he said suddenly. Then he turned and asked the others, 'Which one is the Duchess, the tall dark fella with the cap?'

The lads rolled over doubled with laughter – which is exactly how

Anne, Duchess of Westminster found them the first time she came to see the young Arkle in training.

The 'tall, dark fella with the cap', for the record, was Glen Brown, originally from the Borders and married to a great Cork friend of the Duchess, Dorothy, known as Dobbs.

CQRCR

Young police officer, Garda Cyril Maguire, one of three Guards and a sergeant based in Slane, was seconded in to help at Navan races on Saturday 20 January 1962. Further officers from Duleek and Ashbourne swelled the local Navan force. On this occasion Cyril, who was sometimes posted on traffic duty, was on guard outside the first aid room, ready to move racegoers back and clear the way for an ambulance if or when one should be needed. It was his preferred duty, for it gave him a clear view of the racing.

Little did he, or any of the other spectators that winter's day, guess that they were to witness the start of a legend.

Tom Dreaper's useful mare Kerforo was favourite for the three-mile Bective Maiden Hurdle, the value of which was £133, in ground that was officially described as heavy – for which read 'bottomless' – and stable jockey Pat Taaffe unsurprisingly chose to ride her over the stable's outsider, Arkle. She had won her last three steeplechases, but was eligible for this race because she had never won a hurdle.

As Arkle's work rider, Paddy Woods, with a licence to ride and a number of winners under his belt, hoped he would be given the ride on his charge; he knew better than anyone that the youngster had blossomed and improved since his two bumpers the previous month, and had started to 'show something' for all that his gawky frame had not yet filled out or 'furnished'.

Paddy Woods today admits to feeling disappointed at the time when Liam McLoughlin, who was Kerforo's usual rider at home, was given the nod to ride Arkle instead of him; but Liam was second jockey to the stable and as such he was entitled to be booked.

There are not many maiden hurdles over three miles, and it was felt Arkle was likely to be more suited to the slower pace that the longer race distance would produce. More importantly, it would give him time to see the flights clearly without being run off his immature legs. In other words, it would be an ideal lesson for him.

Trainer's son Jim Dreaper says, 'Even in those days there would have been an assumption that in a race where a trainer had an established odds-on favourite and a youngster running, perhaps the youngster would not be given a hard race.'

A little wintry sun added a touch of warmth, and Paddy Woods himself began this particular January day at Navan by steering Last Link to victory in the three mile chase; Liam McLoughlin was unplaced on Little Horse, and in the day's main handicap hurdle Pat Taaffe was fourth on top-weight Fortria. Fortria had won the previous year's Irish Grand National and fourteen other National Hunt races including Cheltenham's Cotswold Chase (now the 'Arkle'), and Two-Mile Champion Chase (now the 'Queen Mother'), and the inaugural Mackeson Gold Cup at Cheltenham's November meeting (now known as The Open), which he was to win again later that year of 1962.

The Dreaper stable that day in Navan also had high hopes of winning the last race on the card, the Bumper, with Anne, Duchess of Westminster's Ben Stack, who at that stage was considered emphatically superior to Arkle. He was favourite, but finished fourth.

Before that race was off, though, the Duchess's ugly duckling had astounded everyone. Earlier that afternoon, the Duchess asked Pat Taaffe whether she could expect anything from Ben Stack and Arkle.

'Well, Ben Stack might win something pretty soon,' said Pat as revealed in *My Life and Arkle's*, 'but Arkle is still terribly green. At this moment, he just doesn't look like a racehorse to me.'

It was a big field of twenty-seven novice runners and Liam McLoughlin allowed Arkle to run within himself, getting a clear view of the flights on the outside (and therefore actually covering a further distance than other runners) and staying out of trouble. The runners rounded the last bend nearing the end of a stamina-sapping three-mile slog through heavy ground with two uphill flights left. Liam McLoughlin felt 'plenty of horse' under him, gave Arkle a kick and the future wonder horse sliced through the pack; soon only Kerforo and Blunts Cross were ahead of him.

Kerforo, the even money favourite, was at the head of affairs followed by Blunts Cross. Kerforo lost the battle with her rival, ridden by amateur Lord Patrick Beresford, between the last two flights, and Blunts Cross looked 'home and hosed' to the viewers in the stands, to Pat Taaffe now beaten off by him, and to Patrick Beresford himself.

Pat Taaffe was resigned to second place; imagine his surprise, then, when suddenly Arkle swooped by him on a tight rein, to score a sensational first success at odds of 20-1.

'I was astonished. I had seen it happen and I still couldn't believe it.'

As they rode back he chatted with Liam McLoughlin who told him with surprise in his voice that he had been 'just cantering' … 'I just gave him a kick two flights out, that was all, and he began to fly.'

Pat Taaffe recalled in his memoir, '[Arkle] didn't look like a good horse and he didn't move like one either. When I first rode work on him, his action was so bad behind that I thought he would be a slow-coach.'

Lord Patrick Beresford's riding career was limited due to his military commitments; he served with the Royal Horse Guards, the No 1 (Guards) Independent Parachute Company, and R Squadron, 22 the Special Air Service (SAS) Regiment. The son of the Marquess of Waterford, he also made his name as a distinguished polo player. Aged seventy-eight in 2013, he recalls, 'I remember that race very clearly. It was a big field of twenty-seven runners with very heavy ground. Between the last two flights I moved up beside Pat Taaffe, he looked across at me but was beaten, so that left me in front earlier than I would have liked. Blunts Cross started to idle and I was hard at work on him but he wasn't responding; we had almost reached the line when Arkle came whizzing by and won by one and a half lengths.

'At the time I thought I had been unlucky but the form was franked in Fairyhouse at Easter when Kerforo won the Irish Grand National and Blunts Cross won a very competitive handicap chase the next day.'

In amongst the plethora of other riders behind Arkle that day were T.P. Burns, of whom more later (unplaced on Moment's Thoughts), Pat Taaffe's brother Tos (pulled up on Hal Baythorn), and Timmy Hyde on Bidale. Champion NH jockey Richard Dunwoody's amateur father, George, was another who pulled up, on Snow Finch.

A number of years later, Betty Dreaper told me about the race, 'It was over three miles in the mud and we did not then know whether Arkle would get that distance … From the stands we could see one horse on the wide outside passing everything else. It was Arkle and he won as he liked. Tom said, "I think we have got something there."'

Jim says, 'It was the first glimpse of Arkle's real ability.'

೮ಶ೦೩

Before that surprising first win of Arkle's, Liam McLoughlin had already won the Conyngham Cup at Punchestown in 1961 on Little Horse, owned by Colonel Newell of Dunshaughlin, and the Prince of Wales Hurdle, also over banks at Punchestown. Three months after

Navan he was to win the Irish Grand National on Kerforo, by which time any thoughts of her having lost her ability were well and truly debunked.

Liam was aboard her that same year, 1962, when she also won the Thyestes Chase in Gowran Park, the Dan Moore Chase at Thurles and the Leopardstown Chase.

Liam was born and bred in Lagore, Ratoath, close to Kilsallaghan, and after starting his career with Charlie Rogers in County Kildare, he spent fifteen years at Dreapers' before a racing fall at Baldoyle curtailed his riding career in 1967. He was one of the special guests at the opening of the Arkle Pavilion at Navan Racecourse in 2007, and he died in August 2010 at the age of seventy-five.

CRCR

There was plenty of craic in Kelly's Bar in Ashbourne the night of Arkle's first win; now with swish, airy bars, there is one snug bar that has barely altered since that time. The chat in the smoke-filled bar wasn't only about Arkle and the failure of Kerforo; there was also Last Link to celebrate, and Ben Stack to ponder. And, of course, they looked forward to Fortria going chasing again soon.

Kelly's was a haven for horsemen in the 1960s. Greenogue's head lad Paddy Murray would invariably be found there after a winning day at the races. He called everyone 'auld son, he was a lovely man', Cyril Maguire recalls. 'All the lads used to go there, like Joe Finglas, Sean Barker, Nicky O'Connor, as well as Liam McLoughlin and his brother Peter, and former stable jockey Eddie Newman and Greenogue neighbours Al O'Connell and Sean Lynch.'

Paddy Woods, as a non-drinker, was not there but he, too, was as pleased as anyone.

Paddy Woods, now a sprightly octogenarian was Arkle's principal work rider throughout his career. Johnny Lumley, now seventy-eight, was his groom, responsible for cleaning out his stable, strapping (grooming) him and generally tending to his every non-riding need.

It was before the days of mechanical horse-walkers. Instead, there were nearly as many men/lads (no girls/lasses then) as there were horses. Five lads would ride out five or six horses per morning, and there were five more stable lads in charge of them; there were usually about thirty-five horses, in total. The stable lad would bring out the horse and give the work rider a leg up into the saddle, and at the end of the exercise the work rider would hand the reins to the stable lad and move on to the next horse, already saddled and waiting for him. The horse that had just worked was immediately 'dressed over' (sweat brushed off, hooves checked and so on) by the non-riding lad.

Tom Dreaper would walk out with the string, give the riders their instructions, and then wander off to count his cattle and sheep, probably with a bag of grain for the sheep. He would then sit patiently on the Big Stone, probably puffing at his pipe, and watch them cantering by. They would pull up, walk back down, and canter up again. He was an early exponent of 'interval training' long before the term had been coined, for the simple reason that their gallops were limited.

CHAPTER 2

TOM DREAPER – THE QUIET GENIUS

om Dreaper had an equable nature, and the stable was well-managed, the two attributes combining to make for contented staff; the horses sensed it and their well-being benefited.

When Arkle arrived at Greenogue in August 1961 Tom Dreaper's reputation was already in its third decade at the height of the Irish trainers' tree. His star Prince Regent had won the Irish Grand National in 1942, but had to wait to win the Cheltenham Gold Cup until after WWII in 1946; how many times might he have won it but for the war? Horse-racing, like life itself, is littered with 'what ifs'.

By contrast, abandonments due to frost in 1931 and flooding in 1937 sandwiched the five consecutive Gold Cup wins of Golden Miller.

Before Arkle came along, Tom Dreaper had also won the Irish National with Shagreen, Royal Approach (who he rated extra special as he won it as a novice), Olympia and Fortria; (he was to win it five more times, with Kerforo, Last Link, Arkle, Splash and Flyingbolt), so his success with Arkle was no one-off fluke.

This was all a far cry though, from the couple of point-to-pointers the young Tom trained at the far end of the family farm at Donaghmore, County Meath. His family were cattlemen and grass was meant for fattening the cattle; churning it up with shod hooves might not have gone down too well.

They were gentlemen farmers, with enough staff to undertake the manual work, leaving them the leisure to enjoy country pursuits. Thomas William Dreaper was born in 1898, and as he grew up he was surrounded by friends who enjoyed hunting and racing. Tom was first and foremost a cattleman, but nothing would stop him hunting with the Ward Union 'carted stag', riding with dash and verve. His aim was to win the Hunt Cup at the annual point-to-point; not only did Tom win the cup, but so did his son, Jim, and his grandson, Thomas.

James and Harriet Dreaper had another son, Dick and two daughters, Pansy and Connie. At the age of twenty-three Tom moved away from home and set up on his own a mile away in Greenogue, Kilsallaghan; it was a mixed farm of some two hundred acres, roughly divided in half by what was then a quiet road close to the County Dublin border.

Tom used all twenty-five or so fields to train on; some were used for walking, others for cantering, and the biggest one for galloping, and he also had the occasional use of a neighbour's land. There used to be ditches and walk-throughs all over the place and from the start horses had to be adaptable and learn to use their feet. The gallop field, at forty-four acres was much the largest, and five small fields were known jointly as the Hills. Sometimes the horses were boxed over to the beach at Portmarnock, near the old Baldoyle racecourse, between the sea on one side and the dunes that lead over to the golf course on the other.

Tom Dreaper rode with success in point-to-points, winning his first in 1923 on his own Dean Swift; the courses included banks, open ditches and stone walls as well as brush fences. Some of his point-to-point wins were on a mare belonging to Thomas Keppel Henry Kelly, known as Harry, his first outside owner. The mare was called Greenogue Princess and was to become Arkle's grand-dam.

Tom's elder daughter, Eva, remembers him telling her, 'you never changed your hands on the reins from the start of a point-to-point.'

Tom's first win under National Hunt Rules (as opposed to the amateur point-to-point field) came on Mattie's Dream in Navan in 1925 and he continued to ride with success through the 1930s, but a hunter chase at Naas almost finished his career when his horse crashed through a wing. Such a thing happens in a split second: approaching a fence the horse veers unexpectedly to left or right trying to run out, the jockey tries to pull him back towards the fence and the wing intervenes; all this happens at approximately 30mph. Wings were generally made of several horizontal wooden planks rising to six or seven feet high, and to run into one at that speed would probably result in splintered wood, a cut horse and an injured jockey; today's wings are made of flexible white plastic poles. Luckily horses seldom try to run out as most relish jumping, but the result of Tom's mishap left him unconscious for two weeks and in hospital for eight. In time, he rode a few more winners, his last being Prince Regent's first success in a bumper in 1940, but from then on the training took over.

Much of Tom's strict upbringing rubbed off, and for him attendance at church on Sunday was non-negotiable, he also abhorred swearing, while betting remained a lifelong anathema. Tom was also always quietly spoken, but none of that prevented him having a laugh and he could enjoy a good joke with the best of fellows – while his pipe was never far from his side.

Tom was slowly building up a small team, but he might have remained a prime cattle farmer, with the odd point-to-pointer thrown in as a hobby, but for another man's tragedy.

In those days a trainer was a paid servant of the owners of racehorses, and no percentage of prize money, and little kudos for that matter, came a trainer's way. Also, most of the good horses were quickly sold to England. This is what would have happened with his first stars, but Fate intervened.

In the 1930s one Bobby Power of Waterford was breaking and preparing young horses for Mr J.V. (Jimmy) Rank, a British flour magnate. Tragically, Bobby Power was killed in a road accident in 1938 on his way to the Dublin Show and the four horses he had at the time for Mr Rank were transferred to Tom Dreaper, who had caught the owner's eye as a promising small trainer. Once broken, Mr Rank's horses were as usual to be transported to England for their racing careers, but by the time they were ready it was 1939, World War II broke out, racing ceased in England – and the four youngsters remained with Tom Dreaper for training. By the greatest of good fortune, one of those horses was Prince Regent.

Born in 1935, Prince Regent was a good looking, beautifully-proportioned bay gelding by My Prince. Tom Dreaper rode him in his three bumpers, winning the last one in April 1940; Tom Dreaper then hung up his racing boots and Prince Regent was rested until the next year. When he came back the following season he was still growing, but he won two of his three races, at Phoenix Park and Dundalk, with an ease that signalled his developing talent. By this stage Irish horses like him would normally long since have been sold to England or gone there for training, but with the war on all the horses in southern Ireland had to race against each other; it upped the standard but even so, Prince Regent soon began winning races while carrying the big weights that two decades later were to become associated with Arkle.

He won the Irish Grand National in 1942 and four of his other six starts that season and by the end of the war he was considered two and a half to three stone superior to all other chasers in Ireland. It was hoped he would contest the 1945 Cheltenham Gold Cup, but a warble prevented him running. A warble fly larva will get under the skin of a horse, leaving a lump – harmless unless it is under the saddle or girth; in that case, riding the horse would cause severe soreness and probably pus. Warbles have now been eradicated in the UK, Ireland and other European countries.

So Prince Regent had to wait until the following season to run in England; he was first given a trip there to familiarise himself with the stiffer fences and an introduction to a water jump (they were almost never used in Ireland, bar for a brief period in the late 1940s/early 50s in Leopardstown). He duly won a chase in Wetherby in December at odds of 1-10, followed by the 1946 Gold Cup, ridden by Tim Hyde. He also put up two weight-defying performances in the Grand National, finishing third and fourth.

⊗⊗

As the stable began to fill, Tom Dreaper was establishing a stable routine: his staff arrived at 8.30 in the morning (considerably later than in many racing yards), and the horses went out in lots of twos and threes from 9am and once they were fit, they were seldom ridden for longer than forty-five minutes and sometimes only twenty, a comparatively short time compared with many other training establishments; one of the fascinations of racing is that there is a variety of training methods that can produce the same end result.

Jim remembers, 'Of course there were the horrible endless days in the autumn of horseflies, and trotting on the roads for at least an hour.'

The lads had their lunch in the tack room at 12 noon, and horses were groomed between 2-4pm or, if that had been completed in the morning the lads went up to the gallops divoting (replacing with their boot heels clods of grass and earth that had been scuffed out of the ground by the horses' hooves) or cutting furze to replenish the small schooling fences. With the exception of the head lad, Paddy Murray, the men left for home at 4.30. It was longer hours for Paddy Murray who gave the horses four feeds per day, beginning at 7.30am, followed by lunch, tea, and a final feed at 8pm. My sister, Patsy, well remembers him pouring the Guinness into the feed two bottles at a time, one in each hand – but that came later, courtesy of Arkle. Arkle also received up to a dozen eggs in his feed which came from neighbour Sheila Kelly of Greenogue House, (not be confused with Greenogue).

Jim says, 'Of course, it was the less good horses that really needed the eggs and Guinness but they didn't get it – though perhaps the odd pint went for human consumption.'

After 'the Emergency' as World War II is known in Ireland, there was for Tom one missing link. He was forty-nine and an eligible bachelor. His son, Jim, tells of a local tradition of the time: that landowners only got married once they were 'fit for nothing else'. It was time for Tom to go a-courting. Luckily for him, his eye was caught by the eloquent, smartly turned out and elegant Miss Elizabeth Russell who cut a fine figure in the hunting field – and could go with the best – and was equally fetching in the show-ring. It was 1945 and with Prince Regent at his zenith Betty Dreaper, as she became, was to marry the trainer of Ireland's most famous steeplechaser – so far.

Betty was living with her mother, Eva Margaret (née Goodbody), her father, Marcus Russell, having been killed in World War I shortly before she was born in 1915. The Goodbody side of the family were strict Quakers, so they were not initially happy that their daughter was to marry a racehorse trainer! There might be betting – oh dear! They had hoped for someone more 'suitable'.

Marcus Russell came from Moate, County Westmeath from where, coincidentally, Tom Dreaper's longtime head lad, Paddy Murray also hailed. Before the marriage Tom employed a fourteen-year-old lad, Joe Finglas, to 'tidy up the place' before the arrival of the new mistress. Joe stayed for sixty years.

Betty was thirty when she married Tom in St Patrick's Cathedral, Dublin, on 19 June 1945; she became an indispensable part of life at Greenogue, and mother to three fine children – Eva, Jim and Valerie.

Greenogue was a lovely family home for the children to grow up in, full of charm and atmosphere, filled with the paraphernalia of family country life. Small snug rooms move on to large, spacious ones, but still with nooks and crannies here and there. The stables are to one side of the house, and on the far side there used to be a grass tennis court as well as a fruit and vegetable garden. Traffic going past was scant and the number of people around few – the telephone number was Ashbourne 7, the same number as the stable that was to be occupied by Arkle.

Summer holidays were spent down in Waterville, County Kerry, at the Southern Lake Hotel, the trout and salmon-filled waters of Lough Currane lapping at its garden edge. Every year families with pre-teens and teenagers eagerly met up with others of their own age. Eva, Jim and Valerie all swam in the Atlantic rollers, fished for salmon and trout with their mother, Betty, and in the evenings played jolly games with other families. They liked the area so much – renowned for Charlie Chaplin and Gaelic football player and manager the indefatigable Mick O'Dwyer as well as the spectacular scenery and the nearby home of 'the Liberator' Daniel O'Connell at Derrynane – that in time they bought a cottage nearby in Boulakeel, overlooking Ballinskelligs Bay.

Summer breaks were spent there when the mighty steeplechasers were likewise enjoying their summers out at grass; Kelly kettles were boiled, · the children turned into young adults, and Tom, if he had been cajoled there strictly on sufferance, smoked his pipe. He was not a holiday man and preferred to stay in Meath with his horses and cattle. 'Kerrymen spend their lives trying to get out, why should I want to go in?' was his mantra. In later years Jim would take his own three children, Shona, Thomas and Lynsey, down there for holidays, as would Eva, who married Flat trainer Michael Kauntze and had two daughters, Sophia and Nina. Valerie was also a regular visitor and eventual owner.

Jim recalls some childhood pranks at home with his younger sister, Valerie.

'We used to play football on the road … when we were children there used to be one car every twenty-five minutes and one lorry per hour; we devised a game where we wrapped a shoe box in pretty paper and left it in the middle of the road with a fishing line attached to it; we hid in the bushes, the car would stop and the driver would walk back by which time we had retrieved it. We caught a lorry driver twice, then after that he simply drove over the box; next time we wrapped a breeze block with six-inch nails instead, and of course he got a puncture. But he went to Father and that put an end to that.'

αβ

Amongst J.V. Rank's promising horses at Greenogue in the 1950s was Early Mist. Jim tells the story of how this future Grand National winner was taken out hunting, got stuck in a ditch at Palmerstown, adjacent to Greenogue and, with no means of getting him out, was left there; by the next morning he had extricated himself. The experience can't have done any harm for the striking chestnut won his first four races, and the following year won chases at Naas, Fairyhouse and Leopardstown. Mr Rank's three ambitions in life were to win the Derby, the Waterloo Cup (for coursing) and the Grand National. He had finished second in all three but now Early Mist looked his best prospect since Prince Regent for the latter. Unfortunately Mr Rank died, his horses were sold and dispersed, and a year later Early Mist won the 1953 Grand National for his new trainer, a then comparatively unknown Vincent O'Brien (who won the next two as well, with Royal Tan and Quare Times.)

CR CR

My sister Patsy Smiles, née Holland, was about nineteen when she stayed at Greenogue on work experience as a trainer's secretary for a few days. She remembers Tom as a very, very quiet man, she recalls that he said little and that when he did he was so quiet she found it hard to understand him.

He had a pithy turn of phrase; if an agent tried to take the credit for finding him a particularly good horse, say, Tom would simply reply, 'And what about the ones that failed?'

Paddy Woods, Arkle's principal work rider, tells the story of when 'the boss' was queuing to go into the races; there was not a separate turnstile for owners and trainers then. Suddenly the official saw him and beckoned him forward, 'Stand back for the gentleman Mr Dreaper,' he called.

Tom Dreaper did not have a bad temper but he hated to be patronised, and he went white with rage. 'I won't go on, these people are paying and I am going in free – and I am not a gentleman.'

Paddy Woods recalls, 'Where I was reared, with Mr Dreaper, horses weren't put away for the Gold Cup, they ran from October to Punchestown in late April. He didn't overwork horses at home; I reckon other trainers would give their horses more work in two days than ours did in a week. Ours had big heavy feeds whereas other trainers gave lighter feeds that had lots of chemicals.'

He tells a story from a day at Baldoyle when a new steward reckoned the Dreaper runner looked fat. He approached Tom Dreaper in the weighing room before the race and said the horse didn't look fit to run.

Tom Dreaper, smoking his pipe as usual, asked, 'What's wrong?'

'He looks fat,' came the reply.

'Maybe you're right.'

The horse won easily and eventually Tom found the steward. 'He'll be fairly good when he's fit,' he remarked.

On another occasion a lad called Mickey Brien was in Bellewstown when a relation of Arkle's fell and was lying winded on the ground. Tom despatched Paddy Woods to go and look; when he was a hundred yards away the horse got up, but Mickey Brien's eyes were jumping out of his head. It transpired that a cameraman had said he was going to 'shoot' the horse, which Mickey thought meant with a gun, rather than 'shooting' a picture with his camera.

'Only but I went down in time,' he said, 'the baldy cameraman said he was going to shoot him.'

Paddy says he had never seen Tom Dreaper laugh so much as when he heard that.

Arkle appeared one time on the *Late, Late Show* with Gay Byrne, the popular and long-running Irish television chat show. People there were afraid Arkle would go berserk and wreck the place, 'but Arkle would never do such a thing,' Paddy Woods says. 'They put stuff on his feet to stop him slipping and Johnny Lumley brought him in. The boss was no good for small talk. Gay knew nothing about horses and was talking to another guest when Mr Dreaper got up out of his chair and started looking behind the couch. Mr Dreaper told Gay he had been asked to be in a film for Metro Goldwyn Meyer, and when asked in what role he said "to be meself."'

Tom's daughter Eva tells a wonderful story of when Arkle was waiting in the horsebox prior to going on stage: 'A waitress, a Dublin girl, looked at him and said, "He's got real come to bed eyes."'

There was a Dreaper horse called Mountcashel King who twice beat a horse of the Queen Mother's. Tom said, 'she never says how do you do', but on the third time she came over and held out her hand. 'Well done, I am fed up with you. How do you do it?'

Tom told her the horse had been held up at Holyhead for six days, and had only a week at home; he hadn't been sure whether he should come back.

The Queen Mother replied, 'I have a load of them and they will be heading for Holyhead!'

Paddy Woods' son, Francis (Fran), in later years won the Queen Mother Champion Chase (on Klairon Davies in 1996) and as is the custom was invited to the Royal Box afterwards. 'She was some woman. She congratulated him and went through the race,' Paddy says. She asked, 'What happened over the far side? And into the straight you seemed to ease up, why?' Francis explained he had been giving the horse a breather, but what really impressed him was that she had read the race in fine detail.

Francis also twice won the Irish Grand National, in 1994 on Son of War, and two years later on Feathered Gale. Paddy Woods' other son, Eddy, has a thriving horse business in Florida.

'Don't sell cattle north of the border or run horses south of the Thames – or have your wife last thing in the morning in case something better comes along later in the day.' The first half of this joke was told by the Duchess to Tom Dreaper – did she know the ending, Paddy wonders? I expect so.

Tom Dreaper was a wise man; he had very wealthy owners, but his horses always came first. If he felt a horse was not able for a particular race he would not run it. Regardless of what an owner might say, he would turn a deaf ear. Luckily the Duchess was like-minded.

Eva Kauntze says, 'I always remember my father not being happy if one owner had a great number of horses, as he felt that he would not be able to control his own business, and if the owner decided to remove his horses, it would have been financially difficult.'

Among the wealthy English banking owners and the like, Tom Dreaper also trained for the local Baker family, whose Greenogue Princess had been one of his earliest horses; significantly, one of the others he trained for them was the daughter of Greenogue Princess called Bright Cherry, later to become the dam of Arkle.

It was while Bright Cherry was in her heyday that the neighbours' schoolboy son, Ted Kelly, began riding at Dreaper's. The Kellys, at Greenogue House bred good horses themselves and also trained a few, Arkle occasionally working up their gallops for a change of scene.

'Tom was remarkable on a lot of scores,' Ted Kelly says. 'He cut his teeth as a good hunting gentleman, and he traded in half-breds, but when the war came he couldn't sell them. I was still a schoolboy when I was put up on one of them and told to follow him round the farm, jumping little ditches the whole way round.'

During this period Tom Dreaper also used to lend some of these horses to attractive young ladies to hunt, such as Beryl Murless and Leila Brabazon.

In later years, Ted Kelly remembers cantering behind Arkle 'and in his slow paces he was a very bad mover.' But sometimes it happens that a goose can turn into a swan, and Arkle was a prime example of this. Tom was wise enough to know that a good horse can come in many shapes and sizes; he would inwardly digest a horse's performance and then put what he gleaned from that to improve future prospects. As his son, Jim, says, Tom would never have bought a DVD in order to dissect a horse's run even if they had been available.

'His view was that what's happened is in the past, and if something went wrong, move on; I don't think he ever had a cross word with Pat Taaffe [Arkle's main rider] – the most he would say in the paddock was, "I don't think I would ride him the way you did the last day."'

Eva says, 'He kept his thoughts till after schooling on a Monday.'

It is also hard to imagine him having a horse-walker had they been available; today very few yards are without them (Aidan O'Brien at Ballydoyle is one exception, while Dermot Weld, who trains approximately 150 horses has just one, meaning many would never use it).

Tom gave the impression of being unflappable, like his son today, but Jim points out, 'It's a bit like the duck on the pond which is serene on top, but paddling frantically underneath. My father gave no great shows of emotion either in public or at home.'

The biggest regret for Jim is that he didn't know him very well, having been away at boarding school from the age of seven to seventeen.

'I was only home for a total of three months in a year, and then towards the end of his life he was not in very good health.'

Jim was at school at Headford, along with trainer and former jockey Arthur Moore, TV racing pundit and retired auctioneer, Robert Hall, and former top amateur, Jim Wilson; champion Irish jockey Charlie Swan was there later.

Robert Hall remembers, 'Jim was always very modest at school [and still is] including at St Columba's where we went on to. For some reason I had no lessons before 11am on a Saturday and so I would pop out and get an *Irish Field*, then leave it on my desk when I went off for lessons. Somehow whenever I came back it was always gone – Jim had borrowed it.'

One of Jim Dreaper's earliest memories of his father's yard was as a nine-year-old boy when a padded straw ring was made for Fortria to be hobdayed, an operation to correct a wind defect. It was performed by the pioneering Geoffrey Brain from Gloucestershire, and Jim's sister, Eva, who acted as 'theatre nurse' during the operation, remembers that

Geoffrey Brain was a very proud man in the winner's enclosure at Cheltenham when the horse subsequently won there.

Jim also remembers his father's observation regarding tendon injuries, normally to a front leg, and known as 'breaking down.'

He used to tell Jim to count the number of strides a horse took over a hundred yards, and then ask him how many it would be if the stride was shortened by 20 per cent. Nearly always, if a horse had been fired (an operation to try and strengthen a tendon after a horse has broken down), the stride will be slightly shorter and less elastic, and his performance therefore never quite as good again.

His acute observation was a canny attribute. Robert Hall recalls visiting Greenogue as a schoolboy. 'I remember Tom showing me a painting of Fort Leney and Tom asked me what was wrong with it. I didn't know, but it was that in the picture there were divots flying but, he said, that day the ground was good with no divots.'

In 1974, when Jim married Patricia Quirke, Tom and Betty moved into a newly-built house the far side of the yard and, in a seamless move, Jim took over the training, with the bulk of the staff remaining in situ, headed by Paddy Murray.

Tom and Betty knew better than to interfere – and Jim indeed carried on the Greenogue tradition of high class successes including in the Irish Grand National and the Cheltenham Gold Cup – but rather endearingly if Betty was away Tom would come down to the house for tea and cake in the drawing room, brought for him by Patricia at 4pm.

It was also here, shortly before he died in 1975, that he taught his then only grandchild, Sophia, to clap. She was not yet one and was in the playpen and he in his armchair 'minding' her.

CHAPTER 3

'HE WAS SO INTELLIGENT'

With a spirit as inspirational as Arkle's, Miss Alison Baker, daughter of his breeder, Mary Baker, speaks of her determination to walk again at the age of ninety-three. In 2012, she fell in her bedroom as she was putting herself to bed. Fully conscious she found she could not move her legs; one mobile phone was on charge and the other was tantalisingly just out of reach. She had suffered a stroke and remained on the floor for twelve hours until she was found at 10am the next day. After three months in hospital she found on her home-coming that Well Meadow had been transformed by her nieces and friends, freshly painted throughout and made wheelchair friendly; the doors had been widened and a ramp laid to give internal access to the conservatory that has stunning views and will be warm in the summer. The days of living alone and independently are gone, but a brand new exercise bike standing in the corner of her room is testimony to her determination to walk, and when we meet she had been on it twice so far. She has a twinkle in her eye and an infectious girlish giggle. Her faithful chestnut and white collie, Chrissie, and her full time helper, Simone, are discreetly and equally attentive to her every need.

She looks out of the large window at the view stretching across most of Counties Meath and Dublin to the Wicklow Mountains in the distance beyond Dublin, some forty miles away. Across the road behind her smart bungalow the land rises even higher and from there the Mountains of Mourne can be seen. It is in this field that Bright Cherry, Arkle's dam, is buried. Miss Baker left the adjacent home-place, Malahow, and the four hundred acres was split between her siblings after the death of their mother Mary, née Christie, in 1983. Alison was the oldest and has outlived the rest, Dodo, Pidgie, Harry, and June, who came to live with Alison when Harry got married. Pidgie had five daughters and two sons, 'and my nieces are more than good to me,' says Alison.

Malahow has been in the Baker family since Commander Baker bought it some two hundred years ago. They followed the Irish tradition of combining farming with rearing a few thoroughbreds, and selling (usually the geldings) or sometimes racing them (more likely the fillies.) Alison's father, Henry Baker put his mare, Bright Cherry, in training with Tom Dreaper with considerable success. A chestnut by Knight Of The Garter out of Greenogue Princess by My Prince, she won seven chases and placed eleven times from 1948-50 before she retired to stud at the age of seven. For two of her wins she was ridden by Eddie Newman, three by TP Burns, and the last two by Pat Taaffe. One of these was the Drogheda Tradesmen's Chase, Bellewstown which Pat was to win again three years later on another mare, Nas Na Riogh – to become the dam of Arkle's great rival, Mill House.

It has often been said that Bright Cherry could only stay the minimum distance of two miles when the ground was firm, but in fact three of her chase wins were over two and a half miles. However, she certainly was not an out and out stayer, whereas her son Arkle was.

Henry Baker did not live to see Arkle; he died in 1954 three years before the great horse was born and his wife, Mary, continued breeding at Malahow. However, he did have an influence on his being, as Alison remembers with pride.

'It's a pity he never saw him, but he did have an input. He was very keen on Book Law and Archive was out of her, that's why he was chosen, in memory of Dad.'

Archive was not a fashionable sire, having been a dismal failure as a racehorse which resulted in a suitably low stud fee (48 guineas), but he presumably went to stud because he was beautifully bred by the great Nearco out of a Classic-winning mare. Nearco was unbeaten in his native Italy and proved his worth by winning the Grand Prix de Paris and then in particular by becoming an outstanding sire, an attribute continued by his grandson Northern Dancer (and two of his sons, Nijinsky and Sadler's Wells, and two of the latter's sons, Galileo and Montjeu).

Archive's dam Book Law won the St Leger (the long distance Classic) and was narrowly beaten in both the 1,000 Guineas and the Oaks, so she had speed as well as stamina. So, on blood lines, to send a mare to Archive could potentially produce something special ... The extraordinary thing is that although exactly that happened with the breeding of Arkle, lamentably few other good horses were bred by him. (Mariner's Log was one under National Hunt rules and another was a sprinter called Arcandy).

The miracle was that Bright Cherry took to Archive at all.

'She was not a good breeder?' I suggest.

'Oh, she was terrible!'

In fact, Bright Cherry produced two fillies, both by Mustang, in five years at stud before Arkle was born and was promptly barren for six years after his birth, before finally taking to Ballysway, a stallion who was allowed to run free with his mares in the paddock; she then produced two colts in a further eight years at stud, making a total of just six foals in nearly twenty years. Other than Arkle, only one of them, Saval Beg, won just one lowly race. Generally speaking it was the mares of the family who had speed, Arkle proving to be the exception on the male side.

Alison Baker recalls that Bright Cherry was actually sent home by one stud, expelled like a naughty schoolgirl, when she acted more like a stallion with the other mares, biting and kicking them – two characteristics that she emphatically did not pass on to her famous son.

Arkle was born in the early hours of 19 April 1957 at the majestic Ballymacoll Stud in County Meath, where Bright Cherry's next chosen stallion, Straight Deal, stood. Arkle was bay, with black points (lower limbs, plus mane and tail), and there was no white on him. It was a routine, unremarkable foaling, the main thing being that both mother and son were fine, and the little colt was soon on his wobbly legs in the deep straw, with instinct taking him to his mother's milk bar.

Peter Reynolds, now manager at Ballymacoll Stud, was a trainee at Egerton Stud in Newmarket when Arkle was winning his Gold Cups and he gleefully cheered him on. He says, 'There were probably more Mill House supporters there, but Arkle never let me down.

'You could see Malahow from my father's farm in North County Dublin. The Bakers were great friends and I remember seeing my first television in their house. Tom and Betty Dreaper were also great family friends and if I recall I think Eva (Dreaper) was my first girlfriend!

'In 1971 I came to work at Ballymacoll and the then stud groom Danny Daly told me all about foaling Arkle and so I kind of came full circle. We have since foaled a Derby winner North Light in the same box. Alison Baker was here in 1972 and about twenty years ago her car and trailer broke down outside the front gate of the stud so she was back again.

'Yes we are very proud to be, as it says on our website, "The birthplace of Arkle".'

Bright Cherry and her foal stayed there for about two months during which time Bright Cherry was covered several times by Straight Deal without conceiving, and then it was back to the slopes of Malahow, where Arkle roamed for the next three years. On the journey home Arkle somehow banged a hind leg and while not serious, it was bad enough to have the vet, Maxie Cosgrove, called out. He was weaned in the autumn and turned out with other youngsters and a retired hunter; he was well-handled in the winter, coming into a stable and being fed, and once the spring grass came through he stayed out fully again.

Soon after, exactly a year and a day from his birth, Arkle and the hunter tried to reach some escaped fillies on another part of the farm; Arkle got 'hung up' on a strand of barbed wire running through the hedge and cut himself badly. A flap of skin hung down his fore leg and the vet swiftly stitched him up with about forty sutures in all; it healed well but left a life-long scar. The following autumn, Maxie Cosgrove was back, but this was for the routine gelding (castration) operation that almost all National Hunt colts go through.

C3CR

At the age of three the time had come for more formal education. Alison Baker was a great rider to hounds with the Ward Union Stag-hounds and the Fingal Harriers (of which she became a Master), and it was she who gave the young Arkle his first lessons.

'He was the quietest horse ever,' she recalls. 'He was so intelligent. The first day I put on the tack he bucked and kicked so I expected wild things on the second day but no, every lesson simply took one day.

'He was friendly with us and we were to him. He liked a chat, and I talked to him a lot and treated him like the gentleman he became.

'He was a very lucky horse because the Duchess was very fond of him, very, very fond of him.

'And he was well minded by Tom who was very sympathetic. If Arkle had run in the 1963 Gold Cup he might not have been so good later. It is easy to ride a good horse but he still needs minding.

'Arkle and Pat Taaffe were more than jockey and horse; they were good friends, both of them.'

The Sales were held in early August, run in conjunction with the international Royal Dublin Society (RDS) Dublin Horse Show and once the catalogue was printed a number of enquiries were made to the Bakers. One was from former Irish Champion jockeys Tommy 'the Scotchman' Burns and his son, TP Burns who was still riding. TP had not only won on Bright Cherry, but his father had also trained her half-sister Lucca Prince to win the Ladies Cup in Punchestown for his daughter, Stella (TP's sister.)

Father and son travelled to Malahow, hoping to buy the youngster by Archive before the sale, but the Bakers were adamant he should take his chance in the ring.

The Goff's Sales catalogue of Thursday 4 August 1960 for Lot 148 read, 'this gelding has been broken and driven in long reins but not ridden'.

When the Sales day dawned, the CIE lorry arrived at Malahow and the three-year-old gelding was despatched to the Sales; Alison Baker, whose fortieth birthday had been celebrated in April a day after Arkle's third, followed suit. It was the second day of the sale, beginning on Lot 117 which meant Arkle was due to be sold at the start of the second quarter of the day. On the opening day a colt by Archive had fetched £700; this boded well, for the reserve placed on Mrs Mary Baker's gelding was just £500.

During the morning Tommy Tiernan, assisting the Bakers, held the youngster by the headcollar rope as prospective purchasers came into the good-sized, whitewashed stables to view him, to feel his legs, to see him stood up on the concrete outside and let his frame fill their eye.

What they saw was a gawky, unfurnished bay gelding on the weak side standing about sixteen hands high (he was to grow two more inches). When requested Tommy would walk him away, turn and trot back so that they could see how he moved; gangly was probably the best way to describe his stride and the prospective purchasers would look at his breeding once more: useless but well bred sire and a dam who had won seven chases.

The Sales Paddocks stood where the AIB Headquarters is today, opposite the RDS. A railway siding went straight to the paddocks at the city side enabling bloodstock from down the country to travel to and from the Sales by train. The RDS owned the Sales Paddocks (Goff's were tenants) but sold the site in 1973.

Robert Hall says, 'I remember when the old sales paddocks were sold, holes were dug by the purchasers' builders in order to find foundations – they were surprised to find salt water in them when they returned; evidently Ballsbridge isn't far above sea level!'

The RDS also used the Sales Paddocks stabling as an overflow for the Horse Show and Spring Show, and the international showjumpers were also stabled on that side of the Merrion Road, just across the railway line.

Tom Dreaper was one of those who viewed Arkle, and so was the Duchess. These Sales were held during Show week, which guaranteed many visitors, even if some of them were only there to watch and to catch the excitement of an auction sale. Perhaps a few of those, caught up in the atmosphere, found themselves bidding. Others were there, of course, strictly for the buying; trainers, bloodstock agents and owners.

At last Lot 148 was led into the ring. Alison Baker mounted the rostrum and stood just behind the auctioneer, Bob Jeffares, who managed Blackhall Stud for Sir Harold and Lady Zia Wernher. (A granddaughter of theirs, Natalia, is married to the present Duke of Westminster).

The bidding began, and competition was keen. Captain Charlie Radcliffe – who in his time with his Irish friend, Harry Rooney, bought a lot of future jumpers to sell on – was among the bidders, and so was the Duchess of Westminster. To the satisfaction of the Bakers, their youngster fetched more than double his reserve, knocked down to the Duchess of Westminster for 1,150 guineas. Nevertheless, Alison Baker recalls, 'I hated to part with him, but I knew it was inevitable, he was raised for selling.'

She plucked some hairs from his tail before parting and gave them to her mother. Bedridden for most of Arkle's career, she held them tightly each time he ran.

Later in the day the Duchess made a second purchase – the more fashionably-bred and better looking Bray (later Brae) Flame; indeed, the day before he had won an in-hand hunter class at the Dublin Show. That was no mean feat in those days when classes were so full that, after cursory inspection by the judges as the entrants walked around the ring, two rows were lined up, and the 'also-rans' in the back row were not given further scrutiny.

Goff's manager, Michael Hall always took enormous pride in successful Goff's graduates, none more so than Arkle. In later years he was to sell L'Escargot (two Cheltenham Gold Cups, a Grand National and a chase in America) as well as six Grand National winners (Early Mist, Royal Tan, Mr What, Foinavon, Anglo, and Red Alligator), dual Champion Hurdler Monksfield for 740 guineas, and the Derby winner Hard Ridden as a yearling for 270 guineas.

He was followed into the business by his son, Robert, who is now best recognised as part of RTE television racing's double act with Ted Walsh. Probably Robert's most memorable sale was New Approach in 2006 for 440,000 euro; the colt by Galileo (by Sadler's Wells) was beaten a nose in the 2000 Guineas and then won the Epsom Derby.

Robert recalls how, once Arkle had become famous, he would see his father poring over dozens of volumes of the General Stud Book spread out on their dining room table, meticulously researching Arkle's full pedigree going back eight generations.

'It was well pre-internet. Imagine his great joy when he found that the Duchess's hero was in-bred to the first Duke's great horse Bend Or, remote (8x6), but a wonderful coincidence!'

The Duke's grandson Hugh Richard Arthur was born in 1879 and it is said his auburn curls were the colour of the then two-year-old colt, Bend Or, so the baby's lifelong nickname became 'Bendor'. The following year Bend Or – the horse – won the 1880 Derby. (It was claimed at the time that Bend Or had been inadvertently switched as a colt with another chestnut, Tadcaster. In recent years, DNA has proved this to be true, but in any case, the horse racing under the name 'Bend Or' won the race.) The family arms had been *Azure, a bend or*, but they lost them in a lawsuit of 1389 to another claimant by the name of Scrope.

Bendor became the second Duke; in 1947, when he was nearly sixty-eight years of age, he married his fourth wife, Miss Nancy Sullivan from Co Cork – Anne, Duchess of Westminster, to become owner of Arkle.

CHAPTER 4

TRANSFORMING THE DUKE

When the Second Duke of Westminster, Hugh Arthur Richard Grosvenor, and his first wife, Constance (Shelagh) Cornwallis-West, lost their five-year-old son in 1907, the Duke spent the next few decades on a mission to produce another one. Tall, handsome and the richest man in England he may have been, but no amount of money could buy him the son and heir he craved. Marriages, divorces and affairs followed. He had two daughters, Ursula and Mary, by Shelagh, but nothing from wife number two, Violet Rowley, a divorcée with a son of her own. Nor did he have children with wife number three, Loelia Ponsonby, nor with any mistress – Violet's solicitors cited six – among the most notable being French fashion designer and parfumier Coco Chanel.

While the Duke's reputation concerning the treatment of his wives was deplorable, he nevertheless built an excellent rapport with his staff at historic Eaton Hall, Cheshire, at Lochmore in the Highlands of Scotland, at a small sporting estate in north Wales, and at various other residences including Bourdon House in London's Mayfair, and the Chateau Woolsack, Mimizan in France; he also had a permanent suite of rooms in the Hotel Lotti, Paris. He held a good ear in high places, especially with Winston Churchill, a friend since the Boer War, but all the time in his private life he was driven by this elusive desire to produce an heir.

And what an ancient lineage he was trying to preserve: according to the Grosvenor Estate website: 'The Grosvenor family are distantly related to William the Conqueror. Although not direct descendants, an ancient ancestor of the Grosvenor family was Hugh D'Avranches. His nephew was Gilbert le Gros Veneur or "The Chief Huntsman" who was in turn a nephew of William the Conqueror.' This Hugh nicknamed 'Lupus', was to become the first in a line of seven Norman Earls of Chester.

In *Bend'Or, Duke of Westminster,* George Ridley writes, 'At a time when Cecils, Russells and Cavendishes were small farmers or lawyers the Grosvenors were leaders in feudal society. They have remained, settled on their own estates, for the better part of a millennium, in what may be seen as an ideal pattern of the solid continuity of English life.'

In 1945 the Second Duke, now separated, but not yet divorced from his third wife, was toying with buying a property in Ireland because his elder daughter, Ursula, suggested their having an Irish stud to complement that at Eaton Hall, the family seat in Cheshire. Now in his late sixties and still restless, he was walking along a street in Cork city in the company of American Ikey Bell, foxhunter par excellence, when they bumped into a local girl, as recorded by Robin Rhoderick-Jones in *Nancy, The Story of Anne, Duchess of Westminster.*

'Nancy,' said Ikey, 'may I introduce the Duke of Westminster.'

The date was Wednesday 12 December 1945, and Nancy was newly out of wartime First Aid Nursing Yeomanry (FANY) uniform and looking forward to a full season's hunting once more. The day after meeting the Duke, however, she joined his search party for a suitable stud. They looked at and liked a baronial hall called Fort William, with a mile of fishing either side of the Blackwater River, close to Lismore Castle, County Waterford. Nancy invited Ikey Bell and the Duke to stay at her parents' house in Glanmire that night, rather than return to their hotel.

Barely six weeks after the Duke of Westminster bought Fort William, and by dint of superhuman effort by George Ridley, the Duke was ensconced in his new Irish home on 22 January 1946. He arrived to a house filled with flowers arranged at the request of George Ridley (who perhaps was asked to do so by the Duke) by Miss Nancy Sullivan. Two days later, Miss Sullivan not only came to dinner, but also stayed the night. Within a short time she was the talk of the county, much to the disapproval of her parents, not only because the Duke had a scandalous reputation with women, but also because of the age difference of some thirty-six years. From the start Nancy adored him.

George Ridley writes of the period in *Bend'Or*, 'From that time on Bend'Or's life was, for the first time since his youth, happy and relaxed. It was a much less unequal match than any of his previous marriages: all Bend'Or's duchesses were ladies of beauty and character, but Nancy was not only young and high spirited, but a wealthy lady in her own right. On the eve of his marriage to Nancy ... [he] handed me a document which had been brought to him "by a gentleman from London in a black coat and striped trousers."

'The document was a deed making over to Nancy part of the monies of a trust to which she became entitled on marriage. Bend'Or was astonished when he saw the size of the sums involved, and asked "Did you know Nancy was rich? – Good heavens, you don't think, do you, that people will say I am marrying her for her money!"'

They were married on 7 February 1947 and managed to evade publicity by laying a false trail for the Press. Her parents continued to disapprove and although in time her mother, Winifred, relented, it seems her father never did.

The Duchess's first racehorse was Gleam Of Joy, given to her by the Duke, and in 1947 she watched it win at Clonmel – but when it failed to score at Punchestown two weeks later the Duke, according to *Nancy*, suggested 'it should be sold – if not shot!'

Although their marriage was all too brief before the Duke died, the Duchess's influence finally cured the Duke of his wanderlust and brought him the nearest to true contentment in his adult life. She was devoted to him and did anything to please him, agreeing at once to anything he suggested; this usually entailed packing up and moving on yet again at short notice, but finally there was a time when, as described in *Nancy*, as they were driving out of Eaton, this time for a spur of the moment trip to France, he turned to her and said, 'You know, it's very beautiful here.' She agreed. 'Let's not go.' 'Right,' said Nancy – and they didn't; it was as if he had finally found inner peace.

They both adored Lochmore in the Highlands, and loved fishing and stalking – the Duchess was an excellent shot – and it was there, in July 1953 (shortly after they had attended the Coronation of Queen Elizabeth II) that the Second Duke of Westminster, 'Bendor' suffered a coronary thrombosis and two days later died. His young widow was distraught.

Anne, Duchess of Westminster, had been married just six years and was to spend the next half century as one of the richest women in the UK. But she never threw her weight about; she revelled in her charity work; she relished entertaining at Eaton Lodge, she adored fishing, stalking and a rolling wave of entertaining in the Highlands – and she loved racing. The Duke's will provided her with the wherewithal to run various other properties, including the maintenance of the cottages and staff that went with them. Her favourites were Lochmore in Sutherland and Bryanstown in County Kildare; the Duke also took good care of his two daughters, Ursula and Mary.

The Duchess had grown up in Glanmire House, County Cork, the daughter of Brigadier General Edward Langford Sullivan and his wife, Winifred (née Burns). She loved hunting, but when World War II broke out she volunteered for the First Aid Nursing Yeomanry and served for six years as a personnel driver.

A mile away from the Sullivans, the younger Valerie Beamish lived in The Hermitage, Glanmire. From the beer brewing family, she was to show-jump for Ireland and marry renowned bloodstock agent Tom Cooper. Today, Valerie Cooper is a doyenne of Irish racing, as owner, Turf Club member and retired steward, but she well remembers her neighbour Nancy when she was a child and the older man who was courting her.

'Nancy was very good to me as a child, I remember Mrs Sullivan as formidable, and her husband was tall and slim as were both sons. I can remember Colonel [as he then was] Sullivan being able to fall asleep standing bolt upright by a mantelpiece at a dinner party.

'The Duke used to stay, and a horsebox and grooms would come along and take me hunting with Nancy. He was 'Dook' to me, and it was when I was eight to ten years old.

'I remember Nancy's adored brother, Adam, being one of the first men I heard of being killed in the war [in the Norway Campaign]. I often met her other brother George out hacking, he was lovely.'

The Duchess always kept in touch and Valerie used to go to memorable dinner parties at Bryanstown, near Maynooth, where, she remembers, the dining room was lined in silk. On her death, the Duchess bequeathed Valerie a bronze of Arkle.

When Anne, Duchess of Westminster was widowed four years before Arkle was born, she was not only a knowledgeable, accomplished and understanding horsewoman, but she was also wealthy beyond dreams – the perfect position for becoming the owner of the best steeplechaser the world has ever known.

CHAPTER 5

'HE LOOKS LIKE A NEWLY-SHORN SHEEP'

After the Sales at Ballsbridge, Arkle made the first of many journeys across the Irish Sea to the Eaton estate in Cheshire. Anne, Duchess of Westminster had moved from the private wing of Eaton Hall into the newly renovated Eaton Lodge after the Duke's death. There, Arkle roamed the Cheshire parkland – but it transpires he was not the first Arkle to do so. Incredible as it may seem, there was another Arkle, and he was born here on the Eaton Estate.

It wouldn't be possible today, of course, as Arkle's name is protected (see Appendix II), but in 1894 a brown colt by Arklow out of Angelica (whose paternal grand-dam was called Flying Duchess, and his maternal grandsire was King Tom) was born; he was bred by none other than the First Duke of Westminster and he registered his name as Arkle. So Anne, Duchess of Westminster, was not the first to choose the name of one of the mountains on their Scottish Highland estate for a racehorse.

That is where the similarity ends. The first Arkle, I have to relate, showed zero promise: he is known to have run twice, once as a two-year-old over the almost minimum five furlongs, 140 yards in the Prendergast Stakes on the Two Year Old Course at Newmarket on 15 October 1896, for the Duke, and then two years later as a four-year-old at Lingfield Park on 16 September 1898 in a two-mile selling handicap, literally the lowest of the low in flat racing terms, in the name of L. Neumann. On both occasions he finished unplaced. He was then exported to America in 1899, but Andrew B. Chesser of The Jockey Club, Lexington, Kentucky tells me that 'in checking our records available, we could not find any racing or breeding activity to reference for the referred colt in the United States.'

It is known that in 1908, at the age of fourteen, he was moved on once more, this time to Argentina, where it is believed he was a stallion at Haras Las Porteñas and owned by Messrs. R. and O. Guedes, but there the trail ends.

This Arkle's paternal grandsire was the Duke's Bend Or, and in one of those co-incidences in life, not only did the Duke's grandson, the Second Duke Hugh Richard Arthur (nicknamed 'Bendor') go on to marry Nancy O'Sullivan from Cork, who thus became Anne, Duchess of Westminster, owner of *the* Arkle, but also Bend Or appears on both sides of our Arkle's extended pedigree, as researched by the late Michael Hall, manager of Goffs Sales when Arkle was sold there in 1960 to the Duchess.

When 'our' Arkle arrived at Eaton he was stabled at night and his breaking in was finished off by Bill Veal, the groom who was in sole charge of the Duchess's hunters and thoroughbred youngstock.

It was he who backed Arkle and generally further educated him. He was another invaluable cog in Arkle's wheel, a man who played one of the most important parts in Arkle's life, for without his care, skill and patience the youngster could so easily have been rushed and spoilt.

Patience was something the Duchess, Tom Dreaper and Bill Veal all shared, as remembered by Bill Veal's younger daughter, Christina Mercer.

'My father described Arkle, when asked, as a lovely-natured, very steady horse with no malice and very easy to work with.

'He was a wonderful man with a great gift with horses and their care and nurturing was paramount to him. He had endless patience with the horses and was known in the horse world as an expert at what he did.

'My older brother and sister spent a bit of time with Dad but it was me who used to be trailing behind my father worshipping the horses and wallowing in their company. The horses were such a size I couldn't really start riding out with him until I was considered big enough and then I used to ride Her Grace's favourite hunter, Mr Who, whilst my father would be riding alongside with one of the young horses and often leading another. Mr Who was a companion (along with a grumpy mare called Mandarin) to Arkle and all the young horses and was considered, by my father, to be a very steadying influence on them. Mr Who was a truly wonderful horse with a lovely kind and gentle nature, but could produce the goods when called upon to do so (just like Arkle)! He was "The Boss" and certainly didn't like the youngsters edging their noses in front when out exercising.

'I can vaguely remember Arkle (I was born in 1954 so was quite young when he arrived at Eaton). Her Grace always bought her young horses in pairs, shipped them over to Eaton Hall, where my father broke them in and then they would be shipped back to Tom Dreaper for the next stage in their education. It seemed to be a good combination in that the Duchess was a marvellous, understanding and patient owner – and a first-class horse-woman – who relied on the work of my father and Tom Dreaper and never rushed things along – preferring the horses to mature in their own time.'

Christina remembers later in the sixties a film crew arriving to feature her father handling young horses, to demonstrate how he had educated Arkle.

'The film crew wanted to film my father leading the horses from the paddock back to their stables as he would have done with Arkle. These were two young horses at a delicate stage in their training and quite on their toes and when we got back in the stable yard (you will see me trailing behind in the shot as my role was 'crucial'(!) in keeping them moving along) the crew said "bad light – didn't get the shot right" or some such thing, "can you do it again?" and I remember being mortified when my father turned round to them and in a calm, kind but firm voice told them in no uncertain terms that young horses like those could not be messed around, he would do it once more but if that wasn't successful they would have to wait until the following day! He always believed that, like children, horses needed certain things – kindness, firmness and routine.

'I do believe that my father treated each and every one of the horses in his care with the same love and respect, BUT I do not think that he believed that Arkle would go on to be the amazing horse that he eventually became. I know he was immensely proud of being involved with Arkle and he never once had a bet on him (and was actually not a betting man at all) believing that in doing so he might in some way bring Arkle bad luck! My poor mother's suite in our house in Eccleston was nearly wrecked with my father, brother and me jumping up and down whenever Arkle ran – but we were *SO PROUD* of him. I have always felt that Arkle's success was a great "reward" for my father having devoted his working life to caring so devotedly to the horses in his care.

'My grandfather worked with horses too and apparently my father, from a very early age, used to be with him whenever he could (my mother remembers my grandmother telling the story of finding out that my dad was "bunking off school" and going to the stable yard and helping his father and the two of them thought they could keep it quiet from her)! It used to break my heart when it came time for the young horses to leave Eaton to go over to Ireland – and it must have been hard for my father to break the ties with his "charges".'

In the film, Bill Veal said, 'Arkle was a nice colour and had no vice, he was no trouble and very kind, he never bit or kicked. He had great heart room and depth.'

During the summer when Arkle was there, the stable yard at Eaton was being decorated so the horses were moved down close to the Veal's home to some paddocks that were mainly used for the mares and foals from the stud. In the centre of these walled paddocks was a collection of loose boxes where a black and white feral cat used to make his bed in the hay when Arkle was there.

Sadly, Bill Veal died in 1969 at the age of fifty-seven from motor neurone disease; Christina was fifteen years old. She now runs the Albion Inn in the centre of Chester with her husband, Mike.

She remembers, 'Even after my father died (and my mother stayed in our house on the Grosvenor Estate until she died) we kept in touch with Her Grace and she once said to me that she was amazed at how much Arkle's memory was kept alive, commentators on the TV and journalists in the Press comparing other horses with his record. She adored him and it was wonderful that, when he retired to her farm in Ireland, she was able to ride him.'

Christina's nephew, Mark Henshall, visited Dublin as a student in about 1995 and wandered into a picture shop/art gallery. He saw a print of Desert Orchid, Red Rum and Arkle and stood looking at it for a while. The shop owner started chatting and asked if Mark was interested in racing. Mark said that he wasn't but, curiously, had a connection with Arkle because his grandad (who he never met) had broken him in.

Christina says, 'The chap was really interested and there were other people in the shop who joined in the conversation. Mark said they were fascinated to learn of his connection with Arkle and he said that what was so powerful was the fact that this group of people, in a shop he just happened to go into, held Arkle in such high esteem – with reverence almost, they were fascinated! What was memorable for him was the effect the mention of Arkle's name had on everyone in the shop.'

In August 1961 it was time for Arkle and Brae Flame to return to Ireland. The Duchess, who five years earlier had met Tom Dreaper in Leopardstown, had acquired a horse, Sentina, who was already in the yard owned by brothers Alec and Arthur Craigie. Sentina scored a total of two wins and six places. Now, in August 1961, the Duchess offered Tom Dreaper one of her two new youngsters to train. Brae Flame may have had more credentials and been better looking (at that time), but Tom, having won his last point-to-point on Arkle's grand-dam Gree-nogue Princess and trained his dam Bright Cherry to win seven chases, chose the more backward Arkle. Brae Flame went to Willie O'Grady, raced once, broke down and never ran again; such is the lottery of horse racing.

In Tom Dreaper's yard the lads were roughly divided between work riders, who only rode, and grooms, who didn't ride, but mucked out, groomed and generally cared for their charges. Arkle was put in a rear stable behind another one in the back yard and, initially, was tended to by whoever had a free moment at any given time.

Enter fresh-faced teenager Johnny Lumley.

Johnny Lumley's foray into racing lasted just the six years of Arkle's career, but when I met him forty-seven years later he was watching racing on television, following the progress of his fifty cent 'lucky 15' bet in his home near Ratoath, barely a stone's throw from where he grew up in Kilsallaghan and where, at Greenogue, he became known as the luckiest lad in racing.

Although he grew up a mile from the Dreaper's stable where his grandfather, Barney Twomley, had worked, Johnny's first job on leaving school was in a jeweller's shop in the middle of Dublin, where he worked for a year. He then changed direction and worked on a horticultural farm tending bulbs. After six months he came home one evening and said he didn't like it. His grandfather, who lived with the family, suggested he try Tom Dreaper 'and tell him I sent you.' Johnny, aged fifteen and a half, did just that.

'Did he now?' Tom Dreaper mused in his unassuming way on seeing him, probably smoking his pipe. 'Well, you can start on Monday at 8am on the dot, not five to and not five past.'

Johnny Lumley knew nothing about horses, but had been to the local Fairyhouse races with his mother, Molly when he was eleven for the big Easter meeting.

'I had two shillings and put one shilling on Air Prince. I asked my dad and he told me not to but I did and it won at 16-1.'

The next day his mother took him again; he left ten shillings of his winnings at home and took the other seven shillings with him; he promptly got three wins with two-shilling bets on the Tote and won seven pounds. Johnny kept looking at his small fortune in awe but when he got home his mother took it off him.

'But I still had the ten bob from the day before.'

The first time he went racing on his own – to the Irish Grand National at Fairyhouse on Easter Monday – was in 1960, a year before he joined Tom Dreaper's. It was won by Olympia, and Johnny Lumley was soon to learn that a Dreaper horse won it virtually every year in that era – and that his own moment of glory leading up the winner was to come.

'But after my first year at Dreapers, the horses I looked after could never be backed anywhere!'

So although Johnny knew nothing about horse care, he did have an interest in racing when, at 8am sharp on the appointed Monday, he cycled into Tom Dreaper's yard and a job that was to lead to pictures of him in every national paper and on television both sides of the water, usually unnamed, as he led up Arkle. That was in the future. For now he was very much the new boy given whatever humble task might be going.

He knew nothing, but Paddy Murray, the head lad, gave him a fork and told him to muck out an empty stable. Another lad told him to fetch a bale of hay. He was the youngest and the rest used him as much as they could, like a 'gofer' running errands for them. At one time, Tom Dreaper noticed he didn't have a wad (also known as a wisp – a twist of hay used for massaging a horse) in his grooming bag. It turned out he didn't know how to make one, and so Tom Dreaper told him to take a handful of hay home with him and get his grandfather to show him.

Soon the horses went out to grass and the summer was spent in painting the boxes in the red and white that is still re-applied every summer. No more than four horses would be stabled in the summer so by the time autumn came round Johnny still did not have a horse under his care; those that returned to training after their break already had their regular lads.

When Arkle arrived with another new horse belonging to the Duchess he was backward and still in the growing schoolboy gangly stage with legs going out in all directions. He came along with Ben Stack (also owned by the Duchess) who had a glowing reputation and was quickly snapped up by one of the lads to be 'his' horse. It is a tradition in racing yards that lads (and lasses) 'do their two' (or considerably more than two horses each today with fewer staff and the advent of labour saving devices like horse-walkers).

Johnny Lumley says, 'Arkle was just another horse. I was asked to groom him because none of the other lads wanted to. Peter McLoughlin [brother of jockey Liam] rode him out in the afternoon because he was so backward, instead of with the string in the morning.

'One day at home my grandfather asked if I had a horse yet; I told him about the spare horse, Arkle, and he said I should tell them I want him.'

The next day when Paddy Murray asked him to do something with Arkle, the young Johnny replied, 'Yes, but can I mind him?' As none of the other lads wanted him, the answer was a swift 'yes'.

What he found was a gentle horse with natural good manners and a willingness to please; had Johnny Lumley's second horse come as his first there is no knowing how short his career in racing may have been, for Flyingbolt kicked, bit, and would back a person into the stable corner with his bum and hind legs threatening him.

Flyingbolt arrived in the yard less than a year after Arkle, just after a horse called Owens Sedge, who had been bought by film star Gregory Peck specifically to run in the Grand National at Aintree. Here was a case of *déjà vu* – Owens Sedge was quickly bagged by one of the more senior lads because for one thing, a trip to the Grand National was a virtual certainty – and so the wishy-washy chestnut called Flyingbolt became Johnny Lumley's horse – and the one that many people consider the only horse to have been close to Arkle in ability – and this teenage novice lad who had never ridden a horse in his life had the care of them both.

'Flyingbolt never changed or improved in the stable; he always tried to bite and back you into a corner, you always had to be alert.

'With Arkle you could stroll in and sit down in a corner and he wouldn't go out of the open door. He was very placid; I could mess with him like a dog. He would put his head over my shoulder and lick sweets out of my hand, and if I had mints in my pocket he would smell them and try and get at them by poking his head. He was just the same when he was ultra fit as he was when he was fat from grass, there was no difference.'

Johnny Lumley was to lead up Arkle in every single race he ever contested. He relates the feelings of stable lads in general: 'It's not just a horse that you look after, it's different, it doesn't matter who owns, trains or rides it, it's "my" horse; every horse that you mind you consider to be yours, for nine months of the year, seven days a week.

'You don't just go to the parade ring at the races, the whole day is devoted to your horse, whether it's Cheltenham for three or four days, or leaving at seven am to go to Gowran Park taking two and a half hours in a slow box, and you spend the rest of the day with your horse. Once the commentary starts for the first race some horses get excited, so you stay with them. You want your horse to be the best looking so you plait and re-plait; you've no idea what's happened in the other races of the day.

'Leading up a horse I would be talking to him like a human being – at Cheltenham there would be fifty thousand people and you want to keep your horse calm. It's great if you're leading up Arkle, but it's the same with every horse.

'Most grooms walk the course so they know what their horse is facing, not for picking the ground, but to know what it means when they're coming to the fourth last, say, and understand what is still to come.'

When Arkle's first race was still some months away, Tom Dreaper's elder daughter Eva vividly remembers what her father said one day as she sat with him in the Land Rover. They were following the third lot up over the Broadwater River Bridge, along the bumpy farm track, turn in by the two ash trees, embrace low gear and move steadily up the grassy slope of the first of about a dozen fields on that side of the road.

Arkle was at the rear of the third division string.

Tom wiped his brow and turned to Eva. 'What are we going to do with this gangly, gawky creature? He's got no neck, no muscle and looks more like a newly-shorn sheep'.

CHAPTER 6

'THE BIG HORSE' AND ARKLE BEGIN THEIR CAREERS

While Arkle had furthered his education in Cheshire and then was being prepared to run in his first bumper races, another Irish-bred horse was learning his trade with Pat Taaffe's father, Tom.

Although big, the youngster called Mill House did not appear too backward, unlike some bigger horses that are slower to mature. However, a nasty accident left him lucky to be alive, let alone one of the greatest and, in some respects, unluckiest of steeplechasers. How do you call a winner of a Cheltenham Gold Cup, a Hennessy, a King George and a Whitbread Gold Cup unlucky? To have been born in the same year as Arkle, that's how, a view that has been well aired over the years. He won sixteen of his thirty-four races and placed six times; prone to back trouble, he fell a number of times and also acquired leg trouble which, coupled with his size, made him difficult to train. But as a youngster, he was justifiably considered the best, and he made a remarkable come-back to win the 1967 Whitbread Gold Cup, a testament to Fulke Walwyn's training.

Mill House was bred in Naas by the redoubtable Lawlor family. By Prince Hal out of Nas Na Riogh (Irish for Naas) he was raised at Bawnogues Farm, alongside the third last fence in Punchestown, and named after the Lawlors' private house.

'Legs' Lawlor, 6ft 6ins and twenty stone ran the Osberstown House Hotel and Lawlors Hotel, and the house they lived in was called Mill House, where they also did Bed and Breakfast. It was his son, Tom (T.J.) Lawlor who bred the big brown horse with a white star; Bawnogues is now farmed by his son, Ronan. His granddaughter is also known as 'Legs'.

Pat Taaffe not only broke in Mill House for the Lawlors at his home in Alasty, near Straffan, County Kildare, but he had also ridden his dam in all her wins. Together, they won two hurdles and seven chases (the same number as Arkle's dam, Bright Cherry) over two to 2 ¼ miles. Mill House was to be trained by Pat's father, Tom, in Rathcoole, but this was delayed when Mill House put a hind foot through the trailer floor. He skinned his hind leg to the white of the bone, and it was thought at first he would have to be put down. Luckily he recovered, and went into training with Tom Taaffe.

Tom's grandson, Tom, tells the story of when the horse was working before Christmas. Tom Taaffe's three sons, Tos, Bill and Pat were riding work on the horses due to run at the Leopardstown Christmas meeting for whom there were high hopes. A family priest, Father Paddy Fitzsimons, was put up on Mill House and told to sit in with the lads for the young horse to learn something. To the surprise of all, in the last furlong Father Paddy passed the three others and drew five to six lengths clear. Instead of being delighted, the three brothers felt there was no point in going to Leopardstown as intended if the horses could be passed by a raw youngster; but they did and two of the horses won.

As part of Mill House's education Pat Taaffe took him hunting several times, with three different packs, and found him a natural, relishing the wide variety of fences and terrain. Even as a youngster he felt like a powerhouse and came to hand early. He cleared his schooling fences with feet to spare and Pat Taaffe records in his memoir *My Life and Arkle's*, that 'the surge of power was oceanic'. He ran in his first race, a maiden hurdle, in January 1961, finishing fourth, some eleven months before Arkle ever saw a racecourse. Pat Taaffe won Mill House's second hurdle, also at Naas, in March. In April, ridden by Dave Dick, he fell in the Champion Novice Hurdle at the Punchestown Festival, which would have been a big step up in class on what was only his third start so he was obviously promising from an early stage.

Word had spread that here was an exceptional horse, and he was sold to England. When, about a year later, Pat Taaffe heard that his friend Willie Robinson was to ride him, he told him he would be riding the best horse in the world. For a while he was.

Mill House had been bought by UK advertising businessman Mr Bill Gollings who put him in training firstly with Syd Dale, where he again fell in a hurdle, won one, fell in his first chase and won one at Cheltenham. His first jockey in the UK was Ronald Harrison, now eighty-two, who remembers, 'One morning, riding out for Syd Dale, Syd came to me and said Mr Gollings has written a blank cheque and asked me to buy him a horse … Mr Gollings, when seeing the horse, wasn't sure as it was not an attractive horse, Mill House was big and gangly with an ugly head. Mr Gollings eventually bought the horse for £6500.'

In his first race in England Mill House 'buried' Ronald Harrison at the first flight in Newbury. He was third next time and won at Wincanton after which it was thought he might be a Champion Hurdle prospect, but Bill Gollings sent him chasing, firstly at the now defunct Hurst Park. Ron Harrison recalls, 'Unfortunately for me he fell at the water, Mr Gollings had had a bet and was none too pleased. I lost the ride, so they got Tim Brookshaw to ride him at Cheltenham. Soft ground and a novice chase, Tim finds himself full of running and he wins. Mr Gollings send a telegram to Syd at the races, stating "my horse does not win when I have not had a bet." The horse does not go back to Epsom, arrangements were made for him to go to Mr Walwyn in Lambourn. Syd lost the horse.'

This story proves yet again how lucky Arkle was to come from a non-betting stable and to be blessed in his racing career with just one outstanding trainer, one devoted owner and only one jockey in all his chases.

When Mill House moved on to Fulke Walwyn in Lambourn, Willie Robinson was at first retained to ride him and then persuaded to leave Ireland to take up the role of stable jockey, which position he held for nine years. The large-framed Mill House had by now grown in height to 16.3 hands and before long he was to be known as 'the Big Horse.' Although big, he was more precocious than the young Arkle who was to become his nemesis, and he quickly notched up a string of successes. When he headed for the great 1964 Cheltenham Gold Cup contest with Arkle he had won his last six races. He had won at Sandown in December 1962, the 1963 Gold Cup in March, and at Newbury in April. In the autumn he won the Hennessy in November, the King George VI Chase at Kempton and the Gainsborough Chase (under 12 stone 5lbs) in February 1964, so it truly looked as if Pat Taaffe's words were going to be proved right. Certainly, after his 1963 victory his owner proclaimed he would win the next five or six Gold Cups. And then along came Arkle; the clash between the pair in the 1964 Gold Cup remains one of sport's most memorable highlights.

His back problems may have stemmed from his falls, and bigger, heavier horses are often more prone to tendon injuries. Mill House started favourite for both Gold Cups of 1967 and 1968, aged ten and eleven after Arkle had retired, but fell in both. These setbacks, along with having been born in the same year as Arkle, meant that his winning of the 1967 Whitbread Gold Cup, carrying top weight, was one of the most moving sights on a racecourse, a victory he thoroughly deserved.

CB CB

In December 1961 it was decided to let young Arkle take his chance in his first bumper. Betty Dreaper said in an early film clip, 'There was nothing special about him when he first arrived; to begin with he looked moderate.'

The race chosen was the two-mile one furlong Lough Ennell Plate at Mullingar, the track in the middle of Ireland that is now buried under an industrial estate, and which was originally known as Newbrook. In March 1849, a year after the railway had come to the town (and ten years before gas lighting), the Midland and Great Western Railway Company sponsored the Mullingar Steeplechase for £25 at this course, just three years before its final site was opened in 1852. In 1902 the MGWR opened a new railway siding with two separate platforms at Newbrook to facilitate race-goers. This closed in 1929. At the meeting of 18 September 1899, the Kilpatrick Plate over two miles was won by Drumcree, owned by his breeder Charles Hope. He sold him on to Sir Charles Nugent of Ballinlough Castle, County Westmeath for whom he won the 1903 Aintree Grand National, and in 1947 the film *Captain Boycott* was shot at Mullingar racecourse.

In the 1960s Mullingar racecourse was the hub of social life in the Midlands town, yet the final meeting took place on Monday 3 July 1967, six years after Arkle's run there. Vigorous attempts were made to keep the track open by Mullingar singing superstar Joe Dolan and his brother, Ben, but their business proposal for the site was rejected.

On that December day for Arkle's first race in 1961 the ground was characteristically heavy. Seventeen runners were declared, ranging in age from four to eight years and Mark Hely-Hutchinson, an amateur whose father, Lord Donoughmore, had a couple of horses with Tom Dreaper, took the ride. Mark Hely-Hutchinson was a 'Saturday' amateur, generally only available to race on that day because he had a nine-to-five job in the week. He did, however, have an understanding boss at Guinness who allowed him to come in late a couple of times a week, enabling him to ride out at Greenogue first, so long as he stayed on later in the evening.

In time he was head-hunted from the top of Guinness to become director of the Bank of Ireland.

He was to ride thirteen winners in all, including the good mare Olympia, but is under no illusions about Tom Dreaper's view of him.

'He was not unkind, but I don't think he had a high opinion of my riding – I didn't ride enough – but he would put me on some of his horses for bumper races, and he put me on Arkle because he was unfancied, nothing was expected of him.'

He also confesses that he remembers precisely nothing about his two rides on Arkle, but admits he dined out on the story for the rest of his life of being Arkle's only jockey not to win on him. He retired from his brief riding career shortly afterwards, just before his marriage in May 1962. He wanted to ride a horse that had fallen at the last fence in its last three chases. His wife-to-be, Margaret, said she did not want him to go up the aisle in a wheelchair. Pat Taaffe took the ride – and the horse, which simply didn't stay the minimum two miles, again fell at the last fence.

Arkle was one of five four-year-olds in his first race which was won by co-favourite Lady Flame, ridden and trained by Cecil Ronaldson and owned by Mrs C. Ronaldson. Considering how backward Arkle was, his third place in the large field was perfectly respectable, he would have learnt a lot, and his next outing seventeen days later was up a class at the Leopardstown Christmas Festival, on St Stephen's Day (Boxing Day) 1961.

Arkle was third favourite of the ten runners, but he could finish only fourth behind Artist's Treasure, Glyndebourne and, in third, Flying

Wild who he was to meet again in later years.

On board the winner, Kevin Prendergast had 'not a notion' that the horse who was to become the world's best steeplechaser was behind him – which is hardly surprising given that this was Arkle's second ever race and Kevin won it with ease on Artist's Treasure.

'I didn't suspect a future superstar was behind me, I wouldn't even have known he was in the race.'

He does remember the owner of his horse. 'Johnny Wood was a very decent person. He was a big businessman from Cork, and we're still friends; he lives in Florida now.' The trainer was the highly respected Clem Magnier.

Kevin Prendergast, who turned eighty in 2012, is a leading Irish Flat trainer who rode about two hundred winners as an amateur, mainly riding for Paddy Norris, Charlie McCartan, Clem Magnier and Lord Fingal's horses in bumpers for Danny Morgan. He was banned from steeplechasing by his father, P.J. 'Darkie' Prendergast because his Uncle Kevin, Darkie's brother, had been killed at the age of eighteen in a point-to-point at Two Mile House; but one day Kevin took the ride on the dam of Fortria, Senria, in a hurdle in Leopardstown without his father knowing.

'But the next day he saw a picture of me jumping the last; we finished third.'

⚬⚬⚬

Arkle, meanwhile, was considered too slow after his two bumpers so it was decided to enter him for a long-distance hurdle in Navan and continue his education that way. One person, though, knew he had improved a lot at home since those two educational runs; this was Arkle's work rider, Paddy Woods. Paddy was one of the stalwarts of Tom Dreaper's yard; he retired in Downpatrick in 1972 beaten by half a length by

John Harty who went on to ride for him when he became a trainer. Paddy was Arkle's main work rider throughout his career, including the training in 1967 when Arkle got to within a few days of racing again.

'He just came to be my ride out,' Paddy Woods, eighty-three in 2013, remembers. 'I didn't think that much of him at first, he was just another horse. Then one morning I was riding him on the gallop and I thought, "He's going great."

'Pat Taaffe was there and the boss was at the gate. He asked him which horse he wanted to ride in Navan, and Pat chose Kerforo.'

This was hardly surprising, given Kerforo was one of the stable stars and Arkle had yet to show much promise. The stable had a number of runners that day and hopes were high for two or three of them; Arkle, meanwhile, would simply be furthering his education.

Tom Dreaper's horses almost always jumped well and the secret lay in his schooling of them. One of the lads' afternoon jobs was to cut furze to replenish the five small schooling fences, which were placed at irregular distances to teach horses to adapt. Interestingly, Jim Dreaper says furze is a natural wormer for horses, so apart from making excellent fences (horses won't brush through it) it also serves a purpose for horses turned out in the summer on land that contains it.

The man in whose hands Arkle's schooling principally lay was Paddy Woods; born in Fairyhouse and as keen on the GAA (Gaelic Athletic Association) as horseracing, Paddy Woods began work as a lad with Dan Moore, the neighbouring top trainer and former champion rider who was beaten by a short head in the 1938 Aintree Grand National before the advent of cameras.

Paddy Woods remembers Dan's wife, Joan, as 'the best, she is a lady, the best ever; I drove her to the hunt, and she looked after me so well, and gave me food. She was [and is] a lady from tip to toes.'

One day in 1956, Dan Moore let one of the lads go and the other lads walked out in sympathy.

'We all went, and Charlie Reilly, who worked for Mr Dreaper said I should go to him, he was looking for a fellow, but when I went there Mr Dreaper said he didn't want to take me off Dan, but in the end I started on the Monday.'

It was the beginning of two decades at Greenogue, during the early years of which Charlie Reilly was to become Paddy's best man.

At first, in his new job at Dreapers' Paddy was tested. He was given good horses to ride including Spectacular Scot and Wild Delight.

'Spectacular Scot was very strong and the first morning Mr Dreaper asked me if I could manage him. He took a hell of a hold, but I learnt the knack.'

The real test was yet to come, with a horse called Oyster. He was to go down third and canter back still behind. Paddy managed to hold him and Tom told him to go down in front the next time.

'He was trying me, but I rode him in all his races, twice in Mullingar, including a fall – my shoulder still gives me gyp from that today.'

A year after his arrival, Paddy Woods was granted a licence to ride, in 1957. His first race ride was in Mullingar on Woodyard, and he finished second, beaten by Pat Taaffe on Oyster, and Tos Taaffe was third. Oyster was owned by banker George Ansley, who, Paddy remembers, never took a suitcase with him to any country as he had apartments 'everywhere' with sets of clothes in.

Paddy rode his first winner in Navan on The Big Hindu, a horse who was inclined to run away in his races and was wild on the roads.

Tom's daughter Eva recalls, 'The Big Hindu usually had my father flapping his mackintosh to encourage him to conform.'

Paddy learnt to get him relaxed in a race; he 'switched him off' by lobbing (slow cantering) down to the start. It was a twenty-five-plus runner maiden hurdle, but Paddy held the reins loosely and galloped behind. At one point he changed his hands (altered the grip on the reins, which is often taken as a signal by the horse to go faster).

'He was going to run away with me, so I waited until the last flight, popped over and then let him go and he won; it was a great thrill. I also trained my first winner in Navan, Drynamite.'

All this experience was to come into its own once Paddy found himself riding Arkle. The horses were taught to jump as part of their earliest education.

'I rode Arkle every day. He was very good at home. For schooling the boss had them jumping fences upsides from three years old so they knew how to jump fences before they learnt how to gallop. He was a marvellous man for schooling, he would pull them over ditches, and then they were ridden over banks to make them look where they were going. After that, they would trot over a six inch pole on the ground, and increase it to one foot and then two foot.'

Their first experience over the four or five little baby furze fences (which were designed so that they could be jumped in either direction) was off a lunge rein. Once a rider was on he had to sit still and let the horse make his own jumping mistakes.

'They could jump both ways *ad infinitum*, maybe forty times, before they progressed to hurdles,' Paddy says. 'If they hit the top bar it would teach them. Mr Dreaper was a brilliant man, he was a genius; no one knows how good he was.

'I would kick and root into a jump but Mr Dreaper would tell me not to; he would say let him make his own mistakes and learn for himself; it was different in a race, of course, where the jockey often had to help.'

David Tatlow, champion British point-to-point rider for five successive years in the 1960s, used to ride out at Dreapers' when he was staying with Waring Willis at Skryne, County Meath.

'I can see Arkle's head over the door, with a thousand pigeons flying around. It was a magic era.

'Tom was fanatical about water jumps. He used to split open hessian bran sacks, sew them together and bleach them and put gorse under them on the landing side of a gorse hedge, it got the horses to get height over a water jump.

'As I was an amateur, I would get to come into the house for coffee after riding out, with all the silverware, but the professionals had theirs in the tack room with the lads. Pat Taaffe would only come into the house once all the riding lots had finished.

'Tom Dreaper was a wonderful man. We will never see the likes of Arkle again, not just the weight but because then they jumped proper fences, now they are upturned dandy brushes.'

Arkle never fell on the racecourse, but did so once when schooling – well, messing prior to schooling. The horses had gone over to Dan Moore's excellent schooling ground at Fairyhouse, and while waiting for their turn, Pat Taaffe went to pop Arkle over a small hurdle.

'It was too small and he didn't bother jumping it; he caught his toe in the top and came down,' Paddy Woods remembers. 'I think Pat Taaffe broke his collar bone.' (He had stitches in a gash above his eye, according to Pat Taaffe in *My Life and Arkle's*.)

In all his years at Greenogue, Paddy says, 'Mr Dreaper was always a great man to work for.'

A particular instance was when Paddy, with his family growing to eight children, wanted to build a house. Tom Dreaper said he could have a site anywhere on the farm except by his own house. Paddy chose the site up a lane; there was no water but a diviner came and planning permission was granted, however Paddy began to get cold feet. He was 'strapped for money' and wondered what on earth he was doing. He went to Meath County Council to pay a £40 fee and asked what the cost of the site was.

He was told, 'Mr Dreaper has made you a present of that.'

'It was just like winning the lotto,' Paddy says. 'Mr Dreaper minded the building of it as if it was his own; he allowed me half days to check on the workers and he would notice if a ceiling was too high or a gate wrong – he was never wrong.'

Above left: Bend'Or, 2nd Duke of Westminster, in the stable yard archway at Eaton, Cheshire, 1901.

Above right: Anne, Duchess of Westminster, in the robes of a peeress at the time of the Coronation of Queen Elizabeth II, 1953. She was widowed a few weeks later.

Below: Arkle's dam Bright Cherry wins with Pat Taaffe up at Baldoyle in September 1950.

Above: Bright Cherry's grave.

Below: August 1960. Arkle as a three-year-old just about to leave Malahow for Goff's Sales at Ballsbridge, attended by Tommy Tiernan.

Right: Bill Veal, The Duchess's groom (seen here on a young hunter) who backed and further educated the young Arkle at Eaton Lodge.

Below left: Nancy at a meet of the Wynnstay Hounds at Eaton Lodge.
Below right: Tom Dreaper borrows Betty's hunter, Drinagh, for a day with the Wards during the 1948/1949 season.

Above left: Tom & Jim Dreaper in 1958.

Above right: Valerie Dreaper, Sputnik, Tom Dreaper & Arkle.

Left: Valerie shows Arkle her pet lamb.

Above: Arkle with Paddy Woods rounding up sheep on trainer Tom Dreaper's farm at Kilsalaghan, Co, Meath, 8 December 1965.

Below: Arkle started off the 1963-4 season by winning his only flat race in October. He is seen romping home in the Donoughmore Flat race at Navan ridden by TP Burns.

Above: Poetry in motion. Arkle & Pat Taaffe.

Below: The Race of the Century: Arkle beats Mill House in the 1964 Cheltenham Gold.

Above: Arkle and Pat Taaffe on the way to winning the King George VI Chase at Kempton, 27 December 1965.

Below: Flyingbolt, left, and Arkle lead Tom Dreaper's string round a field.

Above: Arkle at his most exuberant in the Whitbread Gold Cup, Sandown 24 April 1965.

Right: Cheltenham Gold Cup, March 1966. The moment Arkle fans held their breaths as Arkle went right through the last fence first time round, yet he did not fall and Pat Taaffe, the consummate horseman, both helped him recover and kept his own balance.

He took the same sort of interest when Paddy started training on his own account.

'He came up to look, just as if I had never left. If you were right with him, he was doubly right with you.

'He was an unbelievably relaxed man; he would sit on the Big Stone and chat with us as we were walking the horses down to the gallops. He would go off to count his sheep and cattle and when we came by again he'd be back sitting on the stone waiting for us.

'He was great with legs and wind and he never tried to buy success. He would buy horses when they looked bad and he could picture them when they looked good.'

Tom Dreaper's reputation was so high that he couldn't bid at a Sales ring because others would be watching – and if Tom Dreaper wanted a horse they would go for it, too.

'He always went for chaser types, though he chose Arkle because he had trained his dam, Bright Cherry; she only stayed two miles and the sire was nothing but Mr Dreaper had such an eye.'

In 2012 Paddy Woods, aged eighty-two, officially retired from his job selling horse feed for Gain, but in fact he still does one or two days a week.

During his career at Dreaper's, Paddy Woods won the Troytown Chase in Navan twice, on Splash and Babysnatcher, but his biggest two suc-cesses were to win two Irish Grand Nationals on Last Link and Splash.

He tells a story from later years when he was getting off the stand in Navan. Someone tapped him on the shoulder and asked, 'Are you the chap who won two Nationals for Tom Dreaper?'

'Yes,' Paddy said.

'Well, any eejit could have.'

C

Back in early 1962 it was time to see how Arkle's home schooling would apply itself on to the racecourse. It was then that he was entered for the three-mile Bective Novice hurdle in Navan, a rank outsider in a field of twenty-seven, with a stunning result, as we have seen.

Arkle's next race after his surprise first win was his first handicap hurdle at Naas (transferred from waterlogged Mullingar) and the distance was over two miles. This was Pat Taaffe's first race ride on him and he started favourite. He won easily enough, beating Soltest by four lengths with Gainstown, ridden by Pat's brother Tos, a further six lengths back.

Pat could not make the weight for the concluding two outings of this, his first season. Arkle's next race was a more valuable affair at Baldoyle, the now defunct seaside course north of Dublin (not to be confused with Ballydoyle in Tipperary where Aidan O'Brien trains). Arkle was on a lower weight (10 stone 1lb) than Pat could manage, so Liam McLoughlin had the ride again. Pat Taaffe rode Fortria, carrying 12 stone 7lbs, and Paddy Woods was on Last Link with the featherweight of 9 stone 3lbs. (Trainers in Ireland have a long-held tradition of switching horses between hurdles and fences, unlike England where it is still comparatively rare; it is a tactic quite often used to 'preserve' a handicap mark, ie before the entries for a big chase close, they would run in hurdles where the form is not taken into account for chases.)

In the event, not one of the Dreaper horses finished in the first four. It was the only time in Arkle's illustrious career that he finished out of the frame (first four places), giving him the ignominious figure 0 in his form, but Baldoyle was a sharp, flat track and Arkle was never able to feature in the two-mile contest.

To conclude the future star's first season, Liam was fourth on him in a two-mile handicap hurdle at the Fairyhouse Easter Festival.

The ugly duckling was not yet a swan and he was turned out for his summer at grass on the Duchess's estate at Bryanstown near Maynooth in County Kildare.

CHAPTER 7

'I HEAR THE HORSE OF THE CENTURY IS GOING TO RUN'

The night of Tuesday 23 October 1962, Maureen Mullins, wife of trainer Paddy, received a telephone call from one of their owners, Tony Onions. He said he wanted to come down early next morning, 24 October, to ride out on his horse Gallant Barney before going on to Gowran Park because 'I hear the horse of the century is going to run.'

This was news to Maureen Mullins, today matriarch to the incredible Mullins dynasty of trainers and jockeys. She recalls, 'I was a bit sceptical and rather surprised; all we really knew at the time was that Arkle had been beaten in a couple of bumpers.'

The President's Handicap Hurdle at Gowran Park was a much more valuable affair than Dundalk where Arkle had opened his second season account.

He had notched a facile win in a lowly two-mile handicap hurdle in Dundalk (now regenerated as Ireland's only all-weather course), at the generous price of 6-1, carrying 11 stone 13lbs with Pat Taaffe up. The favourite was the lowly-weighted Gosley ridden by Timmy Hyde, who remembers,

'I thought I was on a good thing, and between the last two flights I thought I was going to trot up, then I heard this horse [Arkle] coming from behind. I was amazed to be beaten.' Timmy Hyde, now proprietor of Camas Park Stud, Cashel, won many good races in his career including both the Power Gold Cup on the Duchess's Kinloch Brae (trained by Willy O'Grady), and the Jameson Gold Cup on Clusium. He rode against Arkle a number of times but was always beaten, and says, 'He was so bloody good, I hated looking at his tail all the time! He could go on any ground giving three stone away.'

Eight days later Arkle travelled down to Gowran Park, County Kilkenny, home to the Thyestes Chase in January, to the Red Mills Trials Hurdle in February, and the Listed Hurry Harriet race in August and the Group 3 Denny Cordell Lavarack Lanwades Stud fillies' race in September on the Flat. The chairman of the Red Mills feed company is local man Joe Connolly whose great-grandfather founded it; Joe Connolly is also chairman of Gowran Park. It is an attractive, progressive course set in a park-like setting with many trees skirting the wide, undulating track.

Arkle's win at Dundalk had incurred a 4lb penalty, raising his weight to 10 stone 5lbs. Pat Taaffe hoped to ride, but he could not do the weight and Tom Dreaper summoned Paddy Woods to the weighing room.

'He told me I was to ride,' remembers a still-delighted Paddy Woods.

Arkle was the joint-favourite (with Ross Sea) of the twenty-one runners, and Height O' Fashion (who had won the Irish Cesarewitch on the Flat for the Mullins) was top weight on 12 stone.

It wasn't all plain sailing. Paddy had to work hard to get Arkle into a challenging position, and having done so, Arkle knocked over the last flight of hurdles before going on to win.

Paddy Woods recalls, 'Half way through I was pushing and kicking and thought I had no chance, not really. Tripacer with Mick Ennis was going well in front and I began to think I would never get to him. I got serious three out, with slaps down the neck. I asked for a big one, we took off in fourth and landed in the lead, and went clear, but we flattened the last.'

Arkle's brief bumper and hurdling career, only ever a stepping stone to steeplechasing, was over. He was to have one Flat race at the start of his third season otherwise it was only steeplechases from now on, and Pat Taaffe, the tall Kildare man, was on board for all 26 of them; the partnership is now forged for posterity in a truly life-like bronze in Ashbourne.

Pat Taaffe, like Tom Dreaper, was already well established at the top of his professional tree before the gawky new boy Arkle arrived in Greenogue in 1961 and, like Tom Dreaper, he is one of those men about whom one never hears a bad word. He was always modest and humble, quiet and unassuming. Again like his guv'nor he was a man of few words, but those he did utter were invariably wise.

Pat Taaffe was born to be a horseman. His father, Tom, had set off for Australia to make his fortune but returned home penniless a decade later. He took up horse-dealing but also trained a mare for himself called Southern Lass. He won such a large gamble on her that it set him up for life and he became one of Ireland's leading trainers. He and his wife, Kitty had three sons, Bill, Pat, Tos, and two daughters, Lucy (Lou) and Anne; they reared them to be polite, modest and good sportsmen. Their father taught them to ride, and then progressed through show-jumping, hunting and point-to-pointing. In 1936 Pat wanted to enter the Children's Jumping Competition at the RDS Dublin Horse Show, for which the minimum age was ten. Pat, aged nine years and five months, borrowed his elder brother, Bill's, birth certificate (with their father's permission). He jumped four clear rounds on a twenty-year-old piebald pony called Magnolia and was finally beaten – to his chagrin, by a girl – 'a terrible blow to my pride,' as he records in *My Life and Arkle's*. Nevertheless he was awarded a hunting crop for the best performance by a boy under eleven. At thirteen he broke a wrist playing rugby at school. He won his first race on New Year's Day 1946, aged sixteen, and in 1948 he won the Kildare Hunt Cup at Punchestown. A year later, and still riding as an amateur, he rode his first winner for Tom Dreaper, and he turned professional in 1950 following a knee injury the previous year to stable jockey Eddie Newman. In those days, once an amateur became successful and could be seen as a threat to professionals earning their living from racing, they were 'asked' in no uncertain terms by the Stewards to turn professional if they wanted to continue riding. Tom Taaffe was not too happy at the prospect of his son 'hanging round the weighing room looking for rides', but Tom Dreaper assured him he would have the rides for the budding jockey. It was to forge one of the all time great trainer-jockey relationships. In January 1950 Pat's first ride as a professional, by quirk of fate, was on Bright Cherry, to become immortalised as dam of Arkle; although Pat won a number of chases on her, on this occasion the pair finished seventeenth of twenty-one. Pat was riding on the crest of a wave in 1955 when he won the Grand National on Quare Times and the Irish Grand National and the Galway Plate on Umm, but in 1956, a year before Arkle was born, he took such a heavy fall in Kilbeggan, County Westmeath that his career looked over.

He was conveyed to Bon Secour Hospital, Dublin, where it was considered he had only a 50:50 chance of surviving. He was unconscious for five days and only partly conscious for several weeks in hospital after that, but his jockey visitors were not allowed to tell him that he would never ride again. He was in hospital for six weeks, but left vowing to race again. That he did, while still suffering recurring bouts of concussion and amnesia, would not be allowed today. As always, Tom Dreaper was supportive. He booked two rides for him in Manchester; Pat felt he might not do them justice and shouldn't ride, to which Tom replied in that case they wouldn't run. They ran, Pat rode, and both won; Tom's only precaution had been to bring Pat's father over with them.

Pat's wife, Molly, he reveals in *My Life and Arkle's*, said the accident left him with a personality change that lasted for five years.

Had he not recovered sufficiently he would never have ridden Arkle, but jump jockeys are sometimes likened to India rubber balls, and it is incredible how they recover and return to racing. Injuries and hospital are an almost inevitable part of their lives and mercifully the majority are able to continue their chosen path; for most, race-riding is not so much a career as a passion. There was a time, also in the 1950s, when Pat Taaffe was taken to Mullingar Hospital with a broken collar bone and kept in overnight. He received an unexpected visitor next morning.

Michael Murray had ducked off school to go racing in Mullingar, and at the entrance turnstile he overcame the obstacle of having to wear a hat by pulling out his school cap. He was a fan of Pat Taaffe's and, having seen his fall, he borrowed three shillings (15 pence) from his mother when he got home and bought six oranges. He set off with them early next morning and walked from his home near the Green Bridge to the hospital. A porter told him which ward his hero was in, but just as he reached the door a nun emerged and said, 'What do you think you are doing at this hour of the morning? It's not visiting time and you can't come in.'

'Well, I am his cousin,' and the lad walked in.

Michael, now seventy-four, recalls, 'Pat was a lovely, lovely man. He should have been a priest or a pope; he had lovely wavy hair and was about twenty-one. He was a gentleman; we chatted for about fifteen minutes, then Jimmy Cleary, a local amateur rider and his wife came in followed by Eddie Newman. He asked him who I was. I told him my uncle, another Pat Taaffe [no relation], had a butcher's shop in Patrick Street. Then Tos and their father, Tom, arrived in their Plymouth car to take him home so I said goodbye. I met Pat a couple of times after that, and I used to send him Christmas cards, he was my David Beckham.'

Michael moved to England in the late 1950s, but became such a devoted Arkle fan that in later years he named his house in Yorkshire after him.

Another lifelong admirer of Pat Taaffe was much-admired RTÉ broadcaster Colm Murray, who lost his fight with Motor Neurone disease in late July 2013.

'Pat Taaffe was my childhood idol,' he told me a few years ago. 'He was an icon throughout Ireland, every quarter of the country, transcending every sport. He was a superstar, a household name as much as Lester Piggott; he was very warm-hearted and much loved and he had a charisma that endeared him to people. I used to haunt him for his autograph.'

By the time Arkle came into Pat Taaffe's life he was already at the top of the riding tree. He was to win the Cheltenham Gold Cup four times and the Queen Mother Champion Chase a record five times on Fortria (1960, 1961), Ben Stack (1964), Flyingbolt (1966) and Straight Fort (1970). This record was equalled in 2013 by Barry Geraghty: Moscow Flyer twice (2003 and 2005), Big Zeb (2010), Finian's Rainbow (2012), and Sprinter Sacre (2013). Pat Taaffe also won the RSA Chases five times, also a record. Besides Umm in 1955, he won the Irish Grand National on Zonda, 1959, Fortria 1961, Arkle, 1964, and Flyingbolt 1966, and he twice won the Grand National at Aintree, on Quare Times in 1955 and Gay Trip in 1970 shortly before he retired. As a trainer he was to scoop the Cheltenham Gold Cup with the talented Captain Christy in 1974.

Pat's younger brother, Tos, was also a top-flight NH jockey while their older brother, Bill became an accountant. He was at Cheltenham to see all three of Arkle's Gold Cups, and he was there again in 2005 to greet in his nephew Tom Taaffe who trained the winner Kicking King.

Alison Baker says unequivocally, 'Arkle and Pat Taaffe were more than jockey and horse; they were good friends, both of them. Pat Taaffe was very shy, but he and Tom, and later Jim, got on very well.'

CBCR

It was time for Arkle to go steeplechasing. He was already well-schooled and now the finishing touches were given to him. So by the time of his first steeplechase it was old hat to him. Seldom, if ever, was a runner of Tom Dreaper's seen ballooning over a fence or spooking or propping into it. Mind you, the picture of Arkle over the first fence of the Whitbread Gold Cup at Sandown could be called ballooning by the uninitiated, but far from being out of novicey angst, it was simply ebullient, self-assured exuberance.

Paddy Woods now found much horse beneath him; Arkle was taking a keen hold on the gallops and would jig-jog his way there. Increasingly, on his return to his stable, he loved to roll in the long, clean straw put down in readiness for him by Johnny Lumley.

If Arkle had been fairly slow to mature, especially in comparison with Mill House, it was only that horses, like children, progress at different speeds. Tom Taaffe explains, 'Many winners of the Neptune [formerly Sun Alliance hurdle] over two miles, five furlongs at Cheltenham come back to win Champion Hurdles [over two miles], but as four-year-olds they hadn't been put in the two-mile novice hurdle because they were not yet matured enough to cope with the speed. The reality is that you can only go when the horse is ready, he will tell you when he is well, and you try to piece the jigsaw together. A later-maturing horse will not realise his own speed until after the summer break when he is likely to mature physically and mentally – and then suddenly he shows more speed. All good horses have a high cruising speed and can kick pace into that and maintain it; they really only quicken for a hundred yards and keep it for a furlong.'

This is exactly how it happened with Arkle; a promising first season, a summer at grass, growing some more, coming back in the autumn 'tuned in' to racing-stable routine and bang – explosion into the limelight.

Tom Dreaper was confident in the transformation he was seeing in young Arkle. He opted for a novice chase at Cheltenham, no less, for his first run in a steeplechase, the Honeybourne Chase on Saturday 17 November 1962, a two-and-a-half-mile novice supporting event on the Mackeson Gold Cup card, (won by the stable's established star, Fortria.)

Travelling over to the meeting with Pat Taaffe was fellow jockey Timmy Hyde who remembers, 'Pat was very excited about riding Arkle, he was jumping great at home and he believed he was a star in the making.'

It may have been Arkle's first chase, but the lads at Greenogue would not hear of defeat.

Ted Kelly, neighbour of the Dreapers, says, 'You have to put it down to the genius of the man that he took Arkle straight to Cheltenham – but then he was so well schooled at home.'

Jockey Eddie Harty walked into the Cheltenham paddock and doffed his cap to trainer George Spamm and owner Lord Jeffreys. (Descendent of the 'Hanging' Judge Jeffreys, so named for the severe sentences he passed on the 1685 Monmouth rebels who failed in their uprising against King James II. On one day alone at his 'Bloody Assizes' he sentenced 144 men to death; hundreds more were transported to the West Indies.)

Eddie Harty was due to ride Hop On, a five-year-old, in the Honeybourne Chase. Hop On was a fair to middling horse, capable of winning small races and placing regularly. Riding in the 1964 three-day event in the Tokyo Olympic Games and winning the 1969 Grand National on

Highland Wedding were still in the future for the all-round horseman, but he was already established as a professional jockey.

The twelve runners were circling the paddock, the jockeys' mounting bell not yet gone. The trainer began to give Eddie instructions, but as he was doing so the owner piped up with his own request for the jockey.

'I hear there's a horse over from Ireland with a glowing reputation. I want you to see how good he is – take him on.'

The runners filed out on the track, cantered down to the start and at 1.01pm they were off. Eddie Harty tried to obey the orders. He did his best. Half of the runners were five years old and their inexperience showed.

Hop On blundered at the fifth fence. Jomsviking (Jeff King) had fallen at the third and Dargent (Bill Rees) at the sixth. At the notorious downhill fence three out Hop On fell and Eddie Harty was cannoned into orbit, caught on camera by a photographer who had ventured further out than most. He was rewarded with a picture so spectacular that shortly afterwards it graced the front page of the *New York Times*.

The insurgent from Ireland, meanwhile, had sauntered to a twenty-length victory in his first ever steeplechase. Only seven finished and in sixth was the only other five-year-old to complete, Tim Frazer (Stan Mellor).

Ian Balding was also in the race. The talented amateur rider is best known now as a top-drawer Flat race trainer from Kingsclere in Berkshire where some of his gallops run up one side of Watership Down and back down the other. His Derby winner Mill Reef is still considered the best in some quarters.

He recalls that day in Cheltenham: 'I well remember the mighty Arkle's first appearance in England. I rode a useful young chaser called Milo, belonging to Herbert Blagrave. My instructions were to take my time early on, finish well, and to get as close as we could.

'Well, we seemed to be in a different contest to the favourite who already had a lofty reputation. Arkle was always up near the front, took up the running some way from home, and won by a country mile.

'We were too far behind for me to be able to appreciate those trade-mark long, pricked ears or the effortless grace with which he jumped his fences, but we made some late headway to finish third. Milo and I went on to win our next race comfortably, a novice chase at Windsor a few weeks later, and then with only 10 stone 4lbs on his back and ridden by Johnny Haine (I couldn't do the weight), Milo won the Mildmay of Flete handicap Chase at the Cheltenham Festival the following March. So the horse who had finished twenty-four lengths behind Arkle on his debut in England was not exactly a donkey!

'However, I failed to realise at the time that the winner of that novice chase would go on to become, almost certainly, the greatest racehorse of all time – and yes, that does include Mill Reef and Frankel.'

Arkle had run and won three times between 17 October and 17 November, and he was now given a mid-winter break. His next run was in Leopardstown on 23 February.

Located in south Dublin with a view to the Wicklow Mountains, Leopardstown is one of Ireland's smartest tracks. Bringing together town and country, this was the day when Arkle's prowess was seen by a wider home audience.

It was only his second chase, yet he had to carry a whopping 12 stone 11lbs – the biggest weight he ever had in his career, for the two mile event. This wasn't a handicap with a wide range of weights, rather it was a conditions race, with a basic universal weight but with some penalties and allowances, in which Arkle was penalised for his previous wins. Neverthe-less, he showed a clean pair of heels to his pursuers, putting eight lengths between himself and the nearest of his eleven opponents at the line.

There were also a number of English over, looking for opportunities to race, for racing over there was still in the grips of the notorious 1962-63 winter of deep snow; Cheltenham was approaching and the English had been unable to run any of their intended horses.

The weather relented barely a week before the showpiece and so the Irish, whose horses had been able to have preparatory runs and be race-fit were expected to benefit – yet the first four Irish favourites all failed. It was left to Arkle for the last race of the first day to come good in the Broadway (now the RSA) Novices Chase over three miles. There were a healthy fifteen runners and coming down the hill for the last time the race looked far from a foregone conclusion, yet once Pat Taaffe pressed the button that was it: Arkle cruised apparently effortlessly to a twenty-length victory over Jomsviking. It put heart back into the Irish, but this was only an opening day novice chase. All jump racing fans' eyes would be on the Gold Cup on the third and final day for which the six-year-old Mill House was taking on two previous winners of NH racing's highest accolade, the three miles two furlongs level-weighted showpiece.

Very few six-year-olds run in the Gold Cup, let alone win it as Mill House did convincingly, and English viewers truly felt they were seeing the best horse since Golden Miller in the 1930s. Even so, anticipation was already rising on both sides of the water at the prospect of the novice winner Arkle taking on mighty Mill House at a future date.

Arkle, meanwhile, had two more races that spring of 1963, at the prestigious Fairyhouse Easter Festival for the Power Gold Cup, and the Punchestown NH Festival for the John Jameson Cup, both over two and a half miles.

His win in the former meant Arkle had now won his first four chases, but there is nothing unique about that; there have been many other such promising young horses in the past who for one reason or another have simply not gone on to fulfil that high potential. He was still there to have his bubble burst, and for his last race of that season there was a horse so speedy that his rider believed he could be the one to deflate Arkle's growing and glowing reputation.

Silver Green was trained by Joe Osborne and his rider, Alan Lillingston, was in the highest form, having the previous month won the Champion Hurdle on Winning Fair, the first of only two amateurs ever to do so, (the other was Colin Magnier, For Auction 1982.)

Alan Lillingston was convinced Silver Green had the speed to beat Arkle, and he knew a bit about speed.

'Winning Fair was the quickest jumper of hurdles I ever rode; he was like a rocket away from the back of his hurdles.'

It was Wednesday May 1, 1963, the second day of the Punchestown National Hunt Festival. There were just three runners for the John Jameson Cup over two and a half miles and the ground was good. Arkle was 4/7, but Silver Green was only 7/4, which indicated that the seven-year-old might be a match for the rising star. Making up the trio was another seven-year-old Chelsea Set who at 100/7 wasn't totally unconsidered.

Alan Lillingston, now aged seventy-eight, takes up the story:

'Silver Green was very fast and I thought I had a chance; Arkle was only emerging then and I decided to beat him for speed. My horse was a bit free and didn't jump too well behind so at half way I let him go on really fast – but Arkle went by me as if I was standing still.'

Arkle won by fifteen lengths and a distance, and Alan Lillingston's first thought was, 'Here comes a champion.'

Alan Lillingston rode many winners for Tom Dreaper including at one time six in succession, one of which was Flyingbolt. He had the greatest admiration for Tom Dreaper, and loved his dry sense of humour and in particular his one-liners. There was a time he had ridden Flyingbolt in Navan's December meeting.

'Practically every lad in the yard was there, looking to win his Christmas shilling; the ground was heavy and we were going fine but not moving up, we were in the pack so I gave him a smack down the shoulder and he took off with me – we won by nine lengths.'

Tom was not there in the winner's enclosure to greet him in, but as Alan was walking to his car later he heard a familiar voice.

'I want you,' Tom called. Alan walked up to him and Tom asked with a straight face, 'Did you come a bit too soon?'

On another occasion John Lawrence (Lord Oaksey), the most gifted of horse racing writers and himself a top amateur, was staying with the Lillingstons at their Mount Coote Stud in Limerick for some hunting. He enjoyed it so much that he wanted to stay for some more, but he had to write an article for *The Daily Telegraph* by the Tuesday. Alan suggested he call to Tom Dreaper for a visit and thereby stay in Ireland long enough for some more hunting. Jim Dreaper remembers that John Oaksey asked if he could do some schooling, and Tom had replied with one of his one-liners, 'Do you think you'd improve any of them, or would they improve you?' John Lawrence practically dropped his tea cup.

Alan Lillingston recalls that all the Dreaper horses were so well broken and schooled, quite often at Major George Ponsonby's, that they were push-button jobs to ride.

Alan got on well with Tom and the whole set up, but he reserves a special word for his son, Jim, too.

'He won my brother's memorial race [Lord Harrington], and afterwards he wrote the nicest letter to my brother's widow. The racing game is a tough machine and the quieter characters have to be awfully good to make it up to the top.'

Alan Lillingston became a Turf Club Steward and Secretary of the National Hunt Committee; he was involved with the change in the handicapping rules (of which more later), liaising with his opposite number in Britain, Captain Christopher Mordaunt. An all-round horseman, he met his wife, Lady Vivienne Nevill, daughter of the Marquess of Abergavenny from Eridge, Sussex, at the RDS Dublin Show; he was also an international dressage and eventing rider.

CHAPTER 8

THE COMPLETE RACEHORSE

Arkle had run six times in his first season, seven in his second and now, 1963-4, was to be the busiest of his career with eight. His reputation was red hot and the whole of Ireland was on fire about him. England was not. They had their own hero, Mill House, the 'Big Horse' who as a six-year-old had stormed to Cheltenham Gold Cup glory while Arkle was cruising to a mere novice win at the Festival.

The build up on both sides of the water that autumn was intense. Arkle had become what in today's parlance is called a 'Saturday' horse. Television sets were still few and far between in Ireland and many fans, if they could not get to the track, would flock to whatever friends, relations or pubs had this large, new-fangled, somewhat 'snowy' black and white machine taking up a chunk of the sitting room.

At the time Michael Hourigan, now one of Ireland's leading trainers was an apprentice jockey serving his time with Charlie Weld (father of Dermot) at Rosewell House on the Curragh. It was a strict life but a fair one and the lads found Mrs Gita Weld a perfect mother figure. When Arkle was running the lads were allowed into the house to watch him on the television.

'I remember the crowds following him in, people were able to get a lot closer to the horses then,' says Michael Hourigan.

Schoolboy Kevin Colman (now manager of Bellewstown and Laytown races) went to some lengths to reach a television.

'I got the impression that Arkle ran every Saturday – he wasn't wrapped in cotton wool. A family friend, Jim Kelly, ran the local athletics club and worked for the Greenshield stamp people including half day Saturdays. My sister Carmel and I were about twelve and fourteen and we used to go in to Dublin with him; his mother lived in Julianstown and on the way back we would watch Arkle on their black and white telly; television was a great novelty then.'

CRCR

Arkle began his third season by running in a Flat race, against pukka Flat racehorses (unlike his two initial bumpers which are specifically for NH horses in the making.) Although Arkle had gone through the previous season unbeaten (two hurdles and five chases) he was eligible for the one mile six furlong Donoughmore Maiden Plate because he was, indeed, a maiden on the Flat. There were thirteen runners for the weight for age contest; Arkle had to carry 9 stone 6lb along with three others and the lowest weight was 7 stone 13lb; Arkle was odds-on favourite.

It meant he would have to have a flat race jockey. One of the very best professionals was chosen in Tommy 'TP' Burns, who had not only been Champion jockey three times, but who had also grown up with Greenogue very much a part of his childhood.

Speaking in early 2013, just before his eighty-ninth birthday, TP recalled, 'I spent a lot of my childhood at Tom Dreaper's and rode a pony around the yard there. He taught me to drive a motor car and he was a friend. My father, Tommy, hunted with the Wards, and used to ride young horses from Tom when cattle were his number one business and the horses were his pleasure.

'There were some good horses there and they were very carefully trained. They weren't roughed up and half broken down before reaching maturity; he knew how to mind horses, and they would go on racing until they were twelve years old.'

TP rode for Tom Dreaper 'whenever he wanted me' and one of the horses he had ridden for him in the past was Arkle's dam, Bright Cherry.

'Bright Cherry was very good and she didn't go on racing too long, so that she could breed.'

Although mainly known as a Flat jockey TP also rode successfully under NH rules and trained in later years. One horse he trained was Lucca Prince, out of Greenogue Princess and therefore a half-brother to Bright Cherry and uncle to Arkle. The Bakers had sold him because he was very small, but TP won the Ladies Cup at Punchestown with him.

Before Arkle's race in Navan TP popped up to Greenogue and rode out on him.

'He was a bit special and gave me a "proper racehorse" feel. He wasn't unruly or bouncy, but he took a good hold, especially when we'd gone across the road to the gallops. I had a couple of canters on him.'

The Navan race was a midweek fixture, Wednesday 9 October 1963. One of the jockeys in Arkle's race was Tommy Kinane, usually associated with NH racing (he won the 1978 Champion Hurdle on Monksfield), but light enough to ride on the Flat.

'I was on a small little grey mare called Pearl Lady, trained in the North,' he says. 'I remember Arkle being in front of me and I couldn't catch him.'

TP takes up the story: 'Arkle was a horse who liked to come in at his own speed, he couldn't be rushed. Just before we came into the straight

I was getting no feel off him, he was going nowhere with me and I had to get a little bit busy on him, but then he sailed. He was so used to being held up, and he was used to having fences to negotiate, but once he clicked into gear it was all over.

'He was intelligent and knew how to race; a lot of the good ones have that characteristic. If they're too free they'll win a few but not many.'

He remembers the Duchess being there, and everyone clapping. He beat Descador by five lengths, with Pearl Lady a further half length away.

Arkle had proved himself the complete racehorse; the Cesarewitch, a two-mile Flat handicap held in October looked his for the taking after this performance, but Pat Taaffe urged against it, saying it would make him too free when reverting to chasing. This was undoubtedly wise, for Arkle was already beginning to take a healthy hold in some of his races, and a modicum of restraint was imperative when there were thick birch fences four feet six inches high to be negotiated.

The ultimate goal for this season was the Cheltenham Gold Cup in March and already the hype and banter and generally good-natured rivalry between the Arkle and Mill House camps was becoming increasingly vociferous. Arkle had reached his full height of 16.2hh, but more than that, his frame had filled out and he had matured. Even his girth had expanded, but not in the way of beer-bellied men or middle-aged ladies; his physique now showed how much chest room – heart room – he had, not only in the circumference of his girth, but in the width of his chest between his front legs. In addition, he was taking on the air for which he became famed: high head carriage, pricked ears, inquisitive eyes, taking an interest in everything and everyone around him.

First, the two horses were to meet in the Hennessy Gold Cup at Newbury, Arkle having meanwhile sauntered to a ten-length victory in his first handicap chase, the Carey's Cottage chase at Gowran Park in October. In the Hennessy, Arkle finished only third, his first defeat in a chase. It had been a foggy day making visibility poor. Word started going round that Arkle had slipped on landing over the third last, an open ditch, but nobody had been able to see very well. This sounded like the Irish making excuses, although certainly in the pre-race preliminaries Arkle had looked magnificent.

The television recording shows him jumping the fence perfectly, but then the camera returned to the leader, and Arkle's slip on landing was not seen. Pat Taaffe told the Duchess afterwards that he was confident he would have won, but Arkle had landed in a bit of poached ground, which caused the stumble. The going was described as 'very soft' that day and so it will have been churned up by the runners earlier.

One person who did see the mistake close up, says Ted Kelly, was a character from Northern Ireland called John Taylor, an engineering student at the time.

'He was there, down the course, and he told the Dreapers how bad the mistake was.'

At school in England I well remember hearing about the Hennessy (we weren't allowed to watch TV, but we had transistor radios), and the first reaction was, 'Oh, so he's not as good as he's cracked up to be.'

Arkle was to have three more runs in Ireland before the re-match for the Cheltenham Gold Cup, handicaps at Leopardstown, Gowran Park and Leopardstown again, all of them over three-miles. He carried top weight of 12 stone in all three.

Irish racegoers flocked to the tracks and to any television sets they could find; if they failed in both, they resorted to the Pathé News in the local cinema later in the week.

Arkle did not disappoint his growing legions of fans and won all three, although they were not pushovers. For the Christmas Chase, Loving Record made a real fight of it, matching Arkle and actually leading over the last fence before Arkle strode on to a two length victory. He had given the useful grey nine-year-old 29lbs.

It is generally reckoned that 1lb equates to a horse's length in distance, on good ground in a chase. Until recently (within the last decade) when the advent of computerised distances began, a race judge would give a measured result at no more than thirty lengths, after that it became a distance; there was one even longer official distance of 'bad' which went out of use in 1981. The essence of the measurement of a 'distance' came in 1770 when the owner of the great unbeaten horse Eclipse laid a bet that his horse would 'come first and the rest nowhere.' At that time, a horse that was more than 240 yards (a furlong) behind the winner was said to be 'nowhere'. These days, at the other extreme, there is a new measurement of a 'nose', the minimum after a dead heat and shorter than a 'short head.'

The idea behind handicapping is that all horses in the race have an equal chance of winning and, in theory, should reach the winning post in line abreast. Over the centuries trainers and owners have always been out to 'beat the handicapper'; it is said that a horse who wins several races in a short time is 'ahead of the handicapper,' before the handicapper 'catches up with him.'

Ireland has an approachable senior handicapper in Noel O'Brien, who began in 1981 as assistant to Captain Louis Magee, an international horseman and good mentor. Noel O'Brien is always willing to chat with connections about the handicap mark/weight he has given their horse.

'There are plenty of variables, which keeps the job interesting; every race is different. I can just remember watching Arkle on a grainy black and white television and the evocative voice of Peter O'Sullevan.'

Noel O'Brien was only six when Arkle won his third Gold Cup 'but I knew something special was happening.'

He was also influenced by the fact that pupils were given the day off for racing at Punchestown by his national school, and then later three days by his secondary school.

'I was six when I first went to Punchestown and I felt the allure and magic of that time created by Arkle, that's what got me interested in racing.'

Arkle and Loving Record met again next time for the Thyestes Chase at Gowran Park when Arkle gave 31lbs and a ten-length beating to the grey in heavy ground – so roughly the equivalent of giving that good horse a furlong lead at the start. One more pre-Cheltenham race was to come, back at Leopardstown, and once more Arkle had to pull out all the stops as the grey mare Flying Wild matched strides with him until falling at the second-last fence.

Today it is unthinkable that a horse of Arkle's calibre would be running regularly in handicaps; for one thing there are many more conditions races available to the top horses, and for another, such horses are often limited to only a few runs a year, gearing up for Cheltenham; sometimes there are racecourse gallops or even trainers' open days where the stars can be seen going through their paces. It is a gesture for the public, but it is not a substitute for the real thing. For the trainers it is a means to an end: Cheltenham.

Mill House, meanwhile, also remained unbeaten having seen off just two runners in the King George VI Chase at Kempton on Boxing Day and a conditions race at Sandown. He was defending his crown as the winner of his last six races.

The build up was almost over. England would not hear of defeat in the Gold Cup for Mill House; after all, he was not only the reigning champion, but hadn't he already beaten Arkle in the Hennessy? Fulke Walwyn could not conceive of defeat for his mighty chaser. And to his jockey, Willie Robinson, losing was unthinkable.

CHAPTER 9

ENGLAND V IRELAND – AN EPIC GOLD CUP

Willie Robinson was born and reared in Kilcullen, County Kildare, close to where he still lives today with his wife, Susan, née Hall. Willie married Susan the year of this Gold Cup, 1964; her father, Cyril, managed the Irish Stud, not far from where his lifelong friend and rival, Pat Taaffe lived near Rathcoole.

Willie Robinson began his career as an amateur, riding for his father. His first employer was Mrs Peggy St John Nolan, but women in those days were not allowed to hold a trainer's licence, which had to be in the name of her head man (Matt Geraghty). His next retainers were with John Corbett and Dan Moore.

Apart from having already won the Gold Cup with Mill House, Willie Robinson had also won the 1962 Champion Hurdle on Anzio; he was to take the hurdling crown again in 1965 on Kirriemuir, and was to win the Grand National on Team Spirit soon after this pending duel. He rode in the Aintree epic ten times and also won the 1957 Irish Grand National on Kilballyown, having turned professional in 1956, and was Champion Irish jockey in 1958.

So it was not only two great horses, but also two consummate jockeys who were taking each other on at Cheltenham in 1964.

In Ireland fans and connections were equally convinced that victory would be Arkle's. Paddy Woods says, 'I was 150 per cent certain he would win, I couldn't see him being beaten.'

Johnny Lumley is slightly more cautious. 'None of us had been able to see what happened in Newbury and we only had Pat Taaffe's word for it and just hoped he was right. There was a lot of confidence in the Mill House camp.'

In Cheltenham the night before the big showdown, Peter O'Sullevan took the two principal riders out to dinner in the Carlton Hotel (now the Hotel du Vin and Bistro) in Parabola Road.

'During the 1964 Cheltenham Festival, Pat, Willie and I dined together (just the three of us) … with my *Daily Express* column in mind, I asked them to strike a notional bet, the winner of the cup to pay for an exotic holiday for the loser. They were each firmly and seriously convinced that neither Arkle nor Mill House could be beaten.'

Saturday 7 March 1964 and the scene was perfectly set: a mix of sunshine and snow showers bathed Prestbury Park, the huge amphitheatre set beneath Cleeve Hill, the highest point of the Cotswolds. It was one of those occasions when all the pre-race hype lived up to its billing; for many in National Hunt racing the 1964 Cheltenham Gold Cup remains the epitome of the best in steeplechasing.

For much of the winter Mill House had been the odds-on ante-post favourite, at 1-2. There was plenty of Irish money for Arkle who was out to avenge his Newbury slip, but there were even more who could not see why that result should be turned round, so at the off Mill House started at 8-13, and Arkle eased from 6-4 out to 7-4; it was the last time in his life that he did not start as favourite.

It was as good as a two-horse race in spite of the presence of previous Gold Cup winner Pas Seul (back in 1960) who started at 50-1 and King's Nephew who had not only recently won the Great Yorkshire Chase but also, in the canny hands of Stan Mellor, had pounced on and beaten Mill House himself the previous year at Kempton. In spite of this, he started at odds of 20-1.

At school in Eton, Johnny Bradburne (who became a noted amateur rider and husband of Scottish trainer Susan Bradburne) sneaked off to a friendly maid's room to settle down and watch the race.

Memory plays tricks, and having seen a replay of the race many times I feel I saw it live; yet I cannot have done. I was also at school, it was a Saturday (and my birthday – little white china models of horses given by my school pals) and I was almost certainly playing lacrosse that afternoon. My recollection of that is nil, yet of the race it is pristine: Mill House making the running, jumping superbly with his ears pricked; Arkle fighting for his head and being held back forcibly by Pat Taaffe; the water the second time and the pair put some distance between themselves and the other two. Mill House gained ground in the air at the third last, going nearly four lengths clear heading down the hill. Peter O'Sullevan intoned 'and it's the big two now,' and Pat Taaffe's name is being called from the stands.

And the next thing is Arkle just being there, he has moved up imperceptibly and is now poised on Mill House's quarters. He joins him effortlessly at the second last; they gallop round the final bend heading towards the last fence and Willie Robinson goes for his whip. All Pat has to do is shake up Arkle and he goes a length up into the last before drawing clear to a five-length win.

Writing to me in 2013, Sir Peter recalled, 'The special moment? The few seconds when I heard myself offering the words in commentary, "This is the champion. This is the best we've seen for a long time."!'

As they pulled up, the two jockeys leaned across and shook each other's hands.

Racegoers went wild and virtually mobbed Pat Taaffe and Arkle on their way back to the winner's circle, cheering him all the way; the Irish threw their hats up into the air and cheered some more, and thronged into the hallowed enclosure still cheering, a forerunner of things to come twenty-two years later with Dawn Run.

The Duchess of Westminster received the exquisite Gold Cup, Johnny Lumley led Arkle back down the slope to the racecourse stables, and in the jockeys' changing room Pat Taaffe tried to console and commiserate with a forlorn Willie Robinson.

Speaking almost fifty years on when we met at Cheltenham, Willie, wearing a natty rich blue tie with colourful racing motifs, was anxious not to find a reason for the defeat.

He said, 'I always thought there should only be necks between them but Mill House didn't sparkle that day. I don't want to make excuses. Fulke Walwyn couldn't understand; he believed no horse could beat him. Arkle was something special; we knew in our hearts that Arkle was the biggest threat to Mill House.'

The Walwyn camp could barely take in what they had just witnessed: that *any* horse could beat theirs at level weights, let alone by five lengths.

Valerie Cooper, a friend of the Duchess from childhood, was and is also a lifelong friend and annual house guest for Cheltenham of Mill House's trainer, the late Fulke Walwyn and his widow Cath. As usual, she was a guest at their Saxon House, Lambourn, that year and she captures the mood, 'It was a quiet dinner that night. The defeat of Mill House was very disappointing, but Fulke was a professional and just got on with it stoically. The next day was just another day of getting on with things.'

Catching the plane home that night, Tom Dreaper wanted to treat everyone on the plane to a drink.

His elder daughter, Eva, recalls, 'But there was one lady, a wealthy owner, who was already well oiled and she wouldn't sit down. The plane couldn't take off until she did and everyone was looking forward to their drink!

'At 8am next morning my father was out as usual with a bag of corn on his back, on his way to feed the sheep. I know because the Press rang asking to speak to him.'

Life was never quite the same in Greenogue from that day on, though. Overnight, Arkle had confirmed himself superstar status, a pop idol to rival the Beatles, an equine to admire and revere, to pay homage and genuflect to. It never changed. From now on, unexpected callers could arrive at any time of day and by and large Tom Dreaper acquiesced to their requests for a picture with him, or for their child to sit on him, or a hair from his tail. Again, it was a tribute to Arkle's incredible temperament that he took it all in his stride.

Eva remembers, 'One time father put a nun on him, she was the same as a little child having her photo taken with him. Dad could be unpredictable with unannounced visitors, it depended on his humour. One of the visitors was rock star Dickie Rock who wore his winkle pickers, but he was pre-arranged. It wouldn't happen today with security concerns.'

There was a security alert one time. Betty Dreaper answered the phone in the front hall. It was the British Police, warning her that a pair of dopers, masquerading as a couple with the female an attractive blonde, had caught the ferry to Ireland. Betty looked out of the window to the front gates, where just such a couple were getting out of their car.

'They are here right now,' she said.

Paddy Murray stopped them and turned them away, but it was a close shave.

It was also the start of fan letters and they multiplied continuously until such time, eventually, that the Duchess released one of her staff from Bryanstown, Mrs Tinsley, to work one day a week at Greenogue answering such letters; until then, Betty Dreaper had answered each and every one of them herself. Mrs Tinsley stayed twenty years.

Today, cars will slow down several times a day to peer in towards Box Number 7 as they drive past.

CRCR

After that first Gold Cup, Arkle's season was not finished. Three weeks later he contested the Irish Grand National. This was just after the Irish racing authorities, applying an Irish solution to an Irish problem, had come up with the idea of two handicaps, A and B, drawn up when one horse is a stone or more ahead of any other in the entries: A to apply if the top weight should run (Arkle, for example) with the rest compressed two to two and a half stone below him, and B would become a 'normal' handicap, with the weights spread out across the full spectrum, should the top weight not declare to run.

Even before the 1964 Gold Cup, Irish handicaps that had Arkle entered already had him on top weight and the remainder, who would normally be taking up the full weight range, squashed together at the bottom. Captain Magee wrote to the Irish National Hunt Steeplechase Committee and put his case to them, requesting that Rules 40 and 54 be changed. At the time, entries for ordinary races closed three weeks in advance (today it is five days), and the 'Arkle' situation could result in farcical 'handicaps' taking place.

The two rule changes were made on 14 February 1964, in time for the Irish Grand National, and England followed suit and changed their rules not long afterwards.

For many Irishmen, and Dubliners in particular, Easter Monday means only one thing: the Grand National. Fairyhouse lies only a dozen miles from Dublin City Centre and for Dubliners racing there is an annual pilgrimage. This year, 1964, many came simply to cheer Arkle.

Thirteen-year-old Kevin Coleman and his father watched from the infield, along with thousands of others.

'I saw him coming out, and I saw his cap going past the winning post,' Kevin says. 'I remember the crowds. At the time I was more used to going to Croke Park to see Meath playing football; Meath won the All Ireland in 1967, the first time since 1957, the goal was scored by Terry Kearns who these days helps prepare the racecourse at Bellewstown each summer. During Arkle's era he probably had to take second place to football in my life; but Arkle was a Meath horse.'

Arkle gave his customary two to two and a half stone in weight to his six rivals and again one horse made him fight; this was the useful mare, Height O'Fashion, whose rider, Tom Lacy from Rhode, County Offaly, nevertheless remembers: 'She had every chance if she was good enough; there were no excuses – yet she won the principal race at Punchestown, the Guinness Chase by six lengths carrying 12 stone 4lbs.

'Arkle was the real deal,' Tom Lacy says. 'I remember him from his first win in Navan – I was there – and he was always genuine and consistent.'

Height O'Fashion was only 15.3hh, and the previous time she and Arkle had met, in Arkle's last hurdle race in Gowran Park, she had carried 12 stone to his 10 stone 5lbs. She was the same age as Arkle but, like Mill House, had got her career underway earlier and had won her previous race. Now, just one and a half years later in the Irish Grand National, it was Arkle who carried 12 stone and she had just 9 stone 12lbs on her back, such had been Arkle's gigantic progress.

Ted Kelly recalls, 'I remember seeing Height O'Fashion walk into the parade ring and it was a doppelganger moment; bay all over like Arkle and about two-thirds of his size, she was like a smaller model of him, and a complete athlete, she made a huge impression on me.'

Height O'Fashion had to miss the following year's Irish Grand National due to coughing, when she would probably have started favourite, and in 1966 she finished second again, this time to Flyingbolt.

Arkle appeared quite tired at the end of his Irish National, which is hardly surprising, given his weight, the soft ground, the race he was given by the runner up, and the proximity to the Gold Cup. His was the fifth of seven consecutive Irish National winners and ten in all for Tom Dreaper.

Sandwiched either side of Arkle's win were the two ridden by Paddy Woods, in 1963 on Last Link and 1965 on Splash.

Paddy Woods remembers, 'Last Link had a light weight and it was very, very wet and cold. I walked the course the night before with Phyllis and I was feeling miserable, trying to do 9 stone 7lbs. In the race Height O'Fashion went on about two and a half lengths after the second last, I looked beaten, but within fifty yards of the last I revved Last Link, she pinned her ears back and went.

'Height O'Fashion fell at the last and my horse landed on her; we were nearly brought down and came to a standstill, but I caught Liam [McLoughlin on another Dreaper horse, Willow King] just before the post; I still believe I would have won anyway, without Height O'Fashion falling.'

Last Link was not made in the Arkle mould for temperament, for she would kick in the box, lash out at passing cars on roadwork (she once smashed a car headlight) and it was impossible to take shoes on or off her hind feet and she was generally considered to be a witch. But she had the character to overcome adversity and become part of Tom Dreaper's incredible string of Irish National winners.

In 1965 it was the turn of Mr A. Craigie's Splash. It was shortly after Paddy had injured his shoulder and it was touch and go whether he could ride, 'but Mr Craigie was a very loyal owner and I assured him I would be ok.'

It was one of the smallest fields and the favourite was the Charlie Weld-trained Duke of York, third behind Mill House in the 1963 Gold Cup, owned by John Tilling from Sussex.

Paddy was behind the two leaders and alongside Tommy Carberry riding Zonda. Paddy remembers Tommy calling across to him, 'They's going very fast.

'We were a fair bit behind and the others were going like the hammers. Tommy decided to catch up, but I let them go.'

His patience paid off. Splash was 'a bit of a character' who couldn't be hit, and at the fourth last he came off the bit, but Paddy roused him into the third last when fourth of the four runners, landed in the lead and maintained it to the line.

Tom Taaffe remembers the Fairyhouse Festival at which his father retired in 1970.

'I was seven and had been given long trousers as a present but I wasn't allowed to wear them to the races. It was the day before Dad's retirement and I got into a strop about it so I ran away and my parents drove off without me. I ran out to the yard and thought they would holler me back but they didn't.

'I felt emotionally distraught so I decided to leave home and I packed potatoes, carrots and drinks. My nanny, Carmel Rogers, called good luck and I set off across the fields to the canal banks. After about five hours I got bored (I could usually do so after half an hour). When they returned my parents said I got what I deserved. The next day I wore the short trousers, shirt and tie, for Daddy's retirement.

'I liked the hurdy-gurdys and swinging boats; the hawkers were minders to us kids, it was behind the open flat stand near the last fence. Then I was gathered up because Daddy was about to announce his retirement, it was the Tuesday. He didn't go out on a winner, I think he got a fall. It was announced in the weigh room and he was given a presentation; during Punchestown the next month there was a big retirement party at Alasty.

'I was too young to appreciate the Gold Cups, but as the years unfolded and people came for interviews I began to; but it wasn't until I started riding myself that I realised how important they were.'

Pat Taaffe trained a further Gold Cup winner in Captain Christy (as Tom has done with Kicking King), but he was dogged by heart trouble, and died at only sixty-two, in 1992, having undergone Ireland's second heart transplant in 1991.

One of the most important and poignant days in Tom's life was when he gave the homily for his father in the church in Kill. The service was taken by Fr Paddy Fitzsimons (who christened Tom's elder son, Pat after his grandfather). The church was packed and Tom still remembers the funeral 'as clear as day, it meant so much to me.'

The essence of what he said was: 'time has a place for everybody, Daddy had time for everyone.'

He also remembers the Duchess fondly. 'She had a very, very deep voice which shook me at first as a little one, but she always had a chocolate for me. She was terribly good to us. She introduced me to the Queen Mother when I was in my twenties, we had cucumber sandwiches in the royal box; we never had tea, it was always a drink.

'The Duchess was a great lady; owners have to be good people to have horses in training, they are supporting our business. Everyone who has had success in this game at a high level also has had to encounter an awful lot more pain through losing horses or those that turn out to be duds. Brothers and sisters are not the same and this is the reason why so many people become involved, because it is not an exact science. You can increase your chances by buying more expensive lotto tickets, but you are still not guaranteed to win.'

CHAPTER 10

LUMPS OF WEIGHT
AND A CHESHIRE
'HOLIDAY'
1964-1965

In November 1964 Tom Dreaper was at Navan races with runners other than Arkle when he became unwell. A spectator who noticed it was a doctor, Honor Smith of Radcliffe Infirmary, Oxford, sister of one of Tom's owners, Lord Bicester; she recognised it as a stroke. From that moment life for the Dreapers was never the same again. For a start, Betty had to cope with unwanted Press intrusion; she was understandably furious when she found and had to eject a journalist who had tricked his way into Tom's hospital room, and for another she effectively took over the training from then on. But of course it was not just the training, and so Betty got up each day at 6am to see to the family and household chores before starting with the yard at 8am, then back to the office dealing with the secretarial duties as before.

Her daughter, Eva, pays tribute to Betty: 'The admiration and awe of how my mother carried the whole operation was absolutely incredible, especially when one considers how ill my father was and how difficult a time it was. She dealt with it so stoically.'

My sister Patsy had just finished secretarial college and was invited over by Betty to gain experience before becoming a trainer's secretary. Patsy went on to work for Flat trainer Chartres Sturdy in Wiltshire for about three years, where Paul Cole was assistant trainer (he became a leading Newmarket trainer). She also worked for Sussex NH trainer and vet John Hooton.

She remembers, 'Betty was distraught one day because she had not declared something, and she said "you won't learn much from me" but it was just the opposite, she taught me so much in a few days – and I was always extra careful with declarations. Betty was such a lady and so kind.'

While there, Patsy rode out on a cob with Valerie Dreaper, behind the string. Arkle, as usual, was leading them, to keep him settled before he worked, and Patsy particularly remembers his 'I am the king of the castle' attitude.

During his remaining years, Tom had spells of better health, and Eva remembers him looking well in the photographs at both her coming out party in 1966 and for her wedding in 1971. But she didn't like the Russian-style hat he had to wear to keep his head warm after the stroke and she can't bear to see photographs of him in it.

'It reminds me of bad things,' she says.

Eva was at school in Bedgebury Park, Kent, when Arkle ran on two consecutive Saturdays in December 1964, having firstly opened his seasonal account by again winning the two and a half mile Carey's Cottage chase at Gowran Park; he had only two rivals (both on 9 stone 7lbs to his 12 stone) in what was effectively paid exercise.

It was on to the Hennessy at Newbury to make up for the slip that cost him the race the previous year. Arkle was set to carry 12 stone 7lbs; Mill House was now receiving 3lbs from him and with nine runners he did not have to make the running. Arkle, on the other hand, pulled his way to the front in a scintillating display; he made an uncharacteristic mistake six fences from home, and two out he had to fend off the attentions of the lightweight Ferry Boat before surging clear. The Queen Mother's The Rip overhauled and relegated a tired Mill House to fourth place on the run in.

Tom had stayed behind recuperating, and after such a facile race it was decided to keep Arkle in England for the week, at the Duchess's Eaton Lodge from whence he could head for Cheltenham the following Saturday for the Massey Ferguson Gold Cup carrying a whacking 12 stone 10lbs.

So Arkle returned for a week to the care of Bill Veal, accompanied by Johnny Lumley and Liam McLoughlin.

Bill's daughter, Christina Mercer, says, 'I vividly remember that Her Grace said to my father that she wanted Arkle to stay at Eaton to give him a bit of a rest. I can remember looking over the door of his loose box and thinking that he was quite small in stature, but I do remember thinking that he was almost like a film star, so famous and loved was he. He had a couple of "minders" who kipped in the yard.'

What a week in Cheshire that was: for Johnny Lumley and Liam McLoughlin it was a week of nights out drinking, for the Duchess it was an opportunity to show off her star to numerous friends, and for Arkle it was hack-cantering around the estate and being stroked and patted by innumerable admirers in his stable.

Johnny Lumley admits, 'We spent the whole week drinking. There were a couple of hunts, one of them was a lawn meet and we followed in the car. The head man in the stables there had a Morris Traveller with the wooden struts down the sides. We stayed with him, but I can't remember his name [it is unlikely to have been Bill Veal who was older and married at the time]. One night he was in the back of the Morris and fell asleep and we couldn't find our way home from the pub; we drove round and round until 6am until he finally woke up.'

So you didn't get much sleep then?

'We got none! We were young and it didn't matter. But the downside of the week was Arkle getting beaten. I reckon to this day that Mr Dreaper wouldn't have let it happen if he'd been well.'

Arkle had such an equable nature and was so completely race-fit that it is unlikely either the change of scene or the lack of a full gallop accounted for what happened at Cheltenham in a defiant defeat, at least not entirely. It was probably because of the huge burden he had to shoulder in the Massey-Ferguson which, like the Hennessy, was a handicap, combined with coming just too quickly after Newbury, and being over the shorter distance of 2 miles 5 furlongs.

On Massey Ferguson day, 12 December, Tom's daughter, Eva, was in the school play, down in Kent.

'Acting was not my *forte*,' she says, 'and my part was the Irish gardener. I ad libbed; I wanted to finish as quickly as possible, so that I could get to my trannie [transistor radio], and listen to Arkle's race.'

But she didn't make it. In the school hall families who had watched their daughters perform milled around. As Eva was trying to disappear she suddenly heard an English parent interested in racing call out gleefully, 'Isn't it great, the Irish horse has been beaten.'

Eva says, 'I never forgot it, but there was such rivalry then.'

Another time Betty came over for Eva's confirmation, and they went out for lunch, just the two of them, to the Star and Eagle in Goudhurst, a black and white typically Kentish pub set on the steep hill just below the parish church. (It is a pub I remember well because my parents invariably called in on their way home from Kentish point-to-points in the pre-breathaliser days, and my sister and I had to be in the garden.) When Betty and Eva entered that day, the whole room went quiet; everyone else had large post-Confirmation parties, and one was a family of bookmakers.

Eva recalls, 'They were all going "Whishhh" behind their hands. Mum felt that a bit, we stood out like a sore thumb.'

In spite of these incidents I don't believe this was a universal feeling in England where racing fans increasingly took the mighty horse to their hearts; indeed, in time more fan mail arrived from England than from any other country.

Arkle had indeed been beaten in the Massey Ferguson, but his performance in defeat was heroic. There were seven runners including rising star Buona Notte, trained by Bob Turnell and ridden by Johnny Haine, and old rival Flying Wild, trained by Dan Moore and ridden by his son-in-law Tommy Carberry. Interestingly, five of Arkle's rivals had more than 10 stone on their backs, illustrating that this was a good class race. Even so, he was giving two stone plus to all bar Buona Notte to whom he gave 2lbs short of two stone. Arkle didn't know that as he skipped off, pulling Pat Taaffe's arms out, disputing the lead, jumping well and leading from the thirteenth. But he couldn't shake off the attentions of Buona Notte and the mare Flying Wild and they both overtook him approaching the last fence. Here, Buona Notte held a slight lead, but blundered and in as thrilling a finish as it is possible to see up the Cheltenham hill, not only did Flying Wild hold on by a short head, but Arkle himself was responding, gaining with every stride, valiantly defying as best he could the 12 stone 10lbs burden.

Arkle didn't do tame defeat. He was beaten by a length, and there were many who felt this run was as great as any other; and a good few more who felt the handicapper was trying to finish the great horse.

For Tommy Carberry the victory was part of his remarkable career in which the small, wiry Meath man was champion Irish jockey five times. Light enough to ride on the Flat, he was also twice apprentice champion when he was signed on with Curragh trainer Jimmy Lenehan. From there he moved to Dan Moore at Fairyhouse, married the boss's daughter, Pamela and between them they have produced jockeys Paul, Philip, Nina and Peter, and another two sons, Thomas and Mark. He was only twenty when Dan Moore's stable jockey, Willie Robinson, moved to Fulke Walwyn in England, (where he was to be associated with Mill House) and Dan appointed Tommy his stable jockey. Both his first and last rides at Cheltenham brought him wins, in the 1962 Gloucestershire Hurdle on Tripacer and twenty years later in the Arkle Chase of 1982, on The Brockshee for his brother-in-law Arthur Moore. In between, he won the 1975 Gold Cup on Ten Up for Jim Dreaper, and the Irish Grand National twice, on Brown Lad and Tied Cottage.

Never again was Arkle asked to race in such quick succession and after the Massey Ferguson defeat, he did not run again for two and a half months.

He had one prep race before the 1965 Gold Cup, at Leopardstown at the end of February, and he was made to fight hard to beat Scottish Memories, a good two-mile chaser in receipt of 2 ½ stone, by a length.

It was at about this time that dope testing had been started in Irish racing, and vets Ted Kelly (who was also a Turf Club stipendiary steward) and Fred Clarke, whose father had been Keeper of the Matchbook in the 1920s, were appointed to take dope-testing samples from every winner. This is usually done through taking a sample of urine, the horse being encouraged to stale by shaking straw in the stable and whistling. Arkle would have none of it and failed to oblige on every occasion, so a saliva sample was taken instead.

'He treated us with contempt,' says Ted Kelly.

Back in England, Mill House had had to work even harder for his two prep race wins. Even so, once more only two horses lined up against the two stars for the 1965 Cheltenham Gold Cup.

As Arkle entered the paddock he paused, head erect, eyes surveying the scene. When he let Johnny Lumley walk him on the crowds clapped.

He looked magnificent. Spectators crowded against the rails, straining, leaning over to get as close a look as possible. Passing one lady, her arm over the rail, Arkle lent across and neatly took her race card from out of her hand. On the way round, Johnny Lumley retrieved the card from between Arkle's teeth and when they reached the woman again he handed it back to her. She was thrilled.

It was nearly a two-horse race and it might just as well have been, for all that sporting senior Australian three-day event rider Bill Roycroft was making up the numbers on his hog-maned eventer Stoney Crossing at 100-1, along with the 33-1 shot Caduval ridden by Owen McNally for trainer Toby Balding.

The two principals set off side by side, soaring over the first two fences in unison. Arkle was just in front by the third fence and although Mill House once or twice rejoined him, he never headed him. Running down the hill for the final time, Mill House still looked poised to challenge. Were the crowds going to witness a truly thrilling finish? Mill House made a mistake at the third last, trying in vain to match strides with Arkle, but still he moved up again as they raced round the final bend.

Then suddenly it was as good as over. Peter O'Sullevan's commentary describes it: 'And now Arkle opening up now, like a sports car, like a real – as though he's just changed gear! He's opened up, he's changed up, and he's come into the last fence full of running. He's just going to jump it. And a *brilliant* jump! A *superb* jump at the last! Exhibition stuff!

'A fine effort by Mill House but he's absolutely unavailing against the champion. He *is* the greatest, going away to the line, Pat Taaffe riding him out, the horse really enjoying himself. He's given a great exhibition performance this afternoon.'

The winning distances were twenty lengths, and thirty lengths back to a not-disgraced Stoney Crossing, with Caduval nearly a fence behind.

CRORR

Arkle's season was not yet over.

Instead of contesting the Irish Grand National he returned to England for the three mile five furlong season closer, the Whitbread Gold Cup near the end of April. Among the racegoers that day was Michael Kauntze who had just celebrated his twenty-fourth birthday, and was at the time assistant trainer to W.O. Gorman, having learnt initially from Toby Balding, then going on finally to the Flat maestro Vincent O'Brien before becoming a trainer himself in 1975. On that day in Sandown Michael was heading for a career on the Flat, but he had ridden in some point-to-points and he was awestruck by Arkle, firmly believing the great horse covered the back straight over seven fences faster than the colts in the Derby trial the same day. Little did he know then that six years later he would marry the Dreaper's elder daughter, Eva.

The Whitbread was the usual weight range and again only a select few took Arkle on, and of those six, only Brasher made any sort of race of it.

Arkle went in to the first fence in third place, ballooned over it and landed in the lead. Apart from quite a nasty mistake at the downhill fourth fence before the turn into the famous line of railway fences, he jumped superbly. He led round the final bend heading for the Pond fence where Brasher (Jimmy Fitzgerald) again had a crack at him, but up that last hill Arkle stretched once more and won by three lengths, to tumultuous cheers from the crowds.

Michael Kauntze says, 'I have never seen a horse go faster down the back straight in my life.'

The Duchess said on film, 'He really is rather an old show-off, he loves people looking at him.'

CHAPTER 11

FASTER THAN A TRAIN

During the summer Arkle's holiday was interrupted to appear at the Dublin Horse Show, much to the delight of the visitors. Tom Taaffe reveals that he was, in fact, doped for the event. He was given an an ACP tablet just to keep him calm. ACP is a mild sedative (Acetyl Promazine) that is used to reduce anxiety, tension and hyper-excitability, especially for jobs like clipping; as Arkle was not competing it was perfectly legal. This was impossible to tell to those watching for he looked simply magnificent, and one of the best pictures of him is stepping out round the big arena, head held high and almost doing a dressage extended trot, Pat Taaffe in the saddle.

It was then back to Bryanstown, where he was under the supervision of head man Johnny Kelly, before returning to Greenogue for a later than usual start to his season.

Arkle went through the 1965-66 season unbeaten, although there was a stable scare before the first of them. He was entered for the Gallaher Gold Cup, back at Sandown, on November 6.

As usual, Paddy Woods was riding him at home – he reckons he rode Arkle over the bridge above the Broadwater River somewhere between three hundred and four hundred times. By now it was his norm to jig-jog his way out to the gallops, but even when he was at the peak of fitness he never misbehaved.

Paddy Woods remembers, 'No, he would never, ever buck or kick and he wouldn't touch you. There was a day when Johnny was off for a half day and he asked me to do him in the evening. I went in and ran my hands down his legs [checking for any heat which could be a sign of a leg problem]. Arkle jumped – he had been asleep. He hadn't a wrong turn on him.'

Sometimes Arkle was taken up to neighbour Ted Kelly's gallops for a change of scene. Shortly before his trip to England he worked there uncharacteristically badly. Flyingbolt and Liam McLoughlin left Arkle clear behind. Paddy Woods reported as such to Tom Dreaper. About 3pm Tom spoke to Paddy again, and Paddy said that nothing seemed wrong with him. Indeed, Arkle had rolled about ten times, a sure indication, with him, that he was fit. Nevertheless, it meant there was a doubt about running. Then later that day Paddy remembered that Arkle had worked badly on this particular piece of ground before.

'It tumbled me, for some reason he just didn't like the place, and I told the Boss. He said to take him over, [to England] but if he's not right we won't run him. Give him a bit of a canter when you get there.'

'The home work was done and that's what counts,' Paddy says, 'so we trotted on the Thursday and intended to spin on Friday. I asked for another horse to blow with him, and we went to the far side of the course, facing the other way round, intending to canter for a couple of furlongs.

'We were by the railway line when I let him into a canter and just then a train came by. Arkle took off; the train was going very fast, but Arkle was faster, and afterwards he was jumping and bucking around so

I rang the boss, and Arkle was declared for the race.'

What followed the next day was one of Arkle's finest performances.

This was the last time Arkle and Mill House ever met, and the Big Horse was now in receipt of 16lbs, more than a stone, from his old rival. It is a mark of Arkle's superiority, as if any were needed, that an eight-times winner like Candy started at 100-1! Willie Robinson was out injured and David 'the Duke' Nicholson was an able substitute. Word was that Mill House was back to near his best. He had had two runs, second over a short distance to the crack two-miler Dunkirk, and a confidence-restoring facile victory over one rival, whereas Arkle was making his seasonal debut.

It was the only day I ever saw Arkle race live and, armed with my faithful Brownie camera, I watched him walk downhill from the stables, photographed him being led by Johnny Lumley, and followed him towards the paddock. Then it was running to find a place on the lawn and cheering as the big two came out on to the broad sweep of Sandown course. And once they were off, I joined in the breathless, excited 'oohs' and 'aahs' as the two mighty horses matched strides. Candy made the running for the first four fences when Mill House went on, looking great. Arkle, pulling hard, joined him and as they galloped past the crowded grandstands first time he tugged his way to the lead. Both jumped so superbly that they were clapped at each fence, and they were clapped again as they strode by the grandstand and on out for the final circuit.

Mill House was not done with. He eased his way back into the lead along the railway fences last time round, putting four lengths between him and Arkle. The atmosphere changed in the stands. Were we going to see defeat for Himself?

David Nicholson was later to say, 'I saw Arkle and thought – well old chap, we've got you this time. The next moment he was alongside with Pat Taaffe not moving on him ... and then he just changed gear. It broke

Mill House's heart – all the fight went out of him after that.'

It was left to Rondetto to chase Arkle home some twenty lengths adrift, with Mill House four lengths behind him. Had I waited, I would have seen these followed by the Queen Mother's The Rip and Edward Courage's little mare, Lira, but I did not. I joined the mad rush of spectators pouring off the stands – I had a head start by being on the lawn – up parallel with the rhododendron walk and back to the winner's enclosure, there to catch another view of Arkle, sparkling in the November sunshine.

Jim Lewis, later to be owner of Best Mate, says, 'I went to admire Arkle, there was no question of backing him. You could pick him out a mile away because of his enormous presence. I remember most the Sandown race, it was total confirmation of his superiority. I believe this race was his finest hour.'

After it, the commentary to the BBC recording of the race was wiped, and the copy that was sent to RTÉ had music put over it. In 2011, Arkle memorabiliast Nick O'Toole had the tape, minus commentary, and approached Sir Peter O'Sullevan. Sir Peter, aged nearly ninety-three at the time, agreed to come out of retirement to do it; first, he had the tape for three weeks, watching and re-watching the silent race.

'When he told me he was ready, I visited him to record it,' Nick O'Toole says. 'I thought it would take a long time, but he did it in one, he was so professional and had all the homework done.'

The recording was shown at a 2012 charity Cheltenham preview in Monaghan. The room fell silent, and as it finished a standing ovation was given to rapturous applause. Sir Peter had done the recording exactly as if it was live.

Three weeks later, Arkle was back in England, for his third Hennessy. Once again he was given a race of it by Brasher, and it was the one time when Pat Taaffe felt he may have made too much use of his wonderful horse. But win they did, in the end by a healthy fifteen lengths, at odds of 1-6, and carrying his usual 12 stone 7lbs. Three of the eight, John O'Groats, Norther and Game Purston, pulled up when tailed off. Freddie, second in the Grand National to Jay Trump the previous spring, was runner up (10 stone 3lb), Brasher (10 stone) third and last home was Wayward Queen (10 stone 6lb); Happy Arthur fell.

When interviewed after the race the Duchess confirmed that she would not be entering Arkle for the Grand National, for fear of loose horses bringing him down. Pat Taaffe felt the course would not be too dangerous for him. And speaking to me in 2013, Patrick Beresford said, 'Arkle would have won the Grand National standing on his head.'

Interestingly, two 'character' horses of the Duchess's (that is, ones that are 'out of love' with day to day racing, but might rise to a new challenge or occasion) rose to the Grand National test and won the great event. In 1967 Foinavon (after he had been sold), was the sole survivor at the first attempt at the twenty-third fence pile up, and in 1985 Last Suspect won.

Christina Mercer, daughter of Arkle's breaker Bill Veal, recalls, 'After Last Suspect won the National, the Duchess had a party at Eaton Lodge and my mother and I were invited which was lovely. Her Grace loved to share her success with people and I can well imagine her showing off Arkle to people on Eaton Estate, she was so proud of him!'

When Christmas 1965 came around Arkle had already left Irish shores for Kempton Park in readiness for the King George VI chase. But he was not forgotten at home. So many Christmas greetings arrived for him that one tree was entirely given over to his cards.

Boxing Day was on a Sunday and so the race was held on Monday 27 December. Unfortunately the race is remembered by some for the wrong reasons.

At one stage it had looked as if Arkle might have a walk over – handicappers who already found they could not beat him when in receipt of 2 ½ stone were unlikely to try in a conditions event with weights nearly level. Then the sporting Colonel Bill Whitbread entered his top two-miler Dunkirk, 12 stone, 7-1, and the field was completed by Dormant, 12 stone, 25-1 and 100-1 outsider Arctic Ocean, 11 stone 3lbs. Arkle's odds were 1-7.

Dunkirk, with senior rider Bill Rees, set off like a scalded cat, as was his wont and at one stage was a fence ahead, so that viewers began to wonder if he had slipped the field; was a monumental turn over on the cards? After all, Dunkirk was an extremely good two-mile chaser. But, with his style of running, that remained his limit. As Arkle caught up with him at the fifteenth fence Dunkirk almost certainly had an internal haemorrhage *before* he took off. Certainly he was stone dead on landing, with his neck broken and Bill Rees trapped under his body with a broken femur.

Arkle came home in isolation, but the mishap took the edge off his win with some totally misguided people claiming he had killed Dunkirk. He had done nothing of the sort – but it was a tragic end to a brave gesture in running Dunkirk. It transpired later that Dunkirk's lungs had probably been damaged by a recent virus.

In February 1966 Mr Guy Jackson, managing director of Guinness, wrote to Betty Dreaper offering to supply ten dozen bottles of Guinness throughout the season in recognition of the 'kind and pleasant publicity we have had from the association of Guinness with Arkle and your other horses and this is our way of saying "thank you."'

Arkle also received a regular supply of local apples (in addition to carrots and other goodies that fans sent.) Seamus Donnelly from a fruit farm at Nutstown, Garristown, remembers Jim Menton, known as Denny, used to come over from Dreapers for a couple of boxes of apples once a week.

'They were probably Bramley Seedlings; I was in my early twenties; I remember my elder brother was intrigued with Arkle at the time.'

CBCR

There is barely an Irish person of a certain age who does not have his or her own special Arkle memories. He captured the public's imagination on both sides of the Irish Sea, helped initially by the advent of television, but then simply by his sheer greatness.

For twelve-year-old Robert Hall the three-mile Leopardstown Chase was to be his second time watching Arkle. He went with his father, Michael, and he was looking forward to it.

It was also the one and only day that Mrs Mary Baker, Arkle's breeder, saw him live on a racecourse; she had been bed-ridden for most of his career, but she was there that day, in comparative comfort, as a guest of Leopardstown racecourse.

Thousands of people, young and old, poured into Leopardstown; little could they know it would be Arkle's last race in Ireland. He was nine years old and had won twenty-two of his last twenty-four starts. He was utterly in his prime, and in the peak of condition.

He had to give a full three stone to each of his three rivals for the three-mile Leopardstown Chase which he had won for the last two years. The ground was heavy which meant every ounce of lead counted as more. Indeed, the weather had been so bad that not only had the race itself been postponed twice, leaving it running only two and a half weeks before the Gold Cup, but the horses had been held up in their work.

This was before the days of all-weather gallops, and most of Arkle's exercise was undertaken round and round ordinary, fairly small grass fields. Occasionally he would go for a racecourse gallop or, as we have seen, up to neighbour Ted Kelly, and once or twice the horses were boxed over to the sands at Portmarnock, about fifteen miles away, but Paddy Woods believes Arkle never went there, probably because it didn't tie in with his race schedule.

So Arkle was short of a serious gallop; the same could have been said for his three rivals although two of them, Height O' Fashion (J.P. Sullivan) and his stable companion Splash (Paddy Woods) had run more recently than him on the course. The field was completed by Packed Home (Tommy Carberry). Although all three received a whopping three stone, none were slouches; Height O'Fashion had finished a close second to Arkle in the Irish Grand National, Splash had won that race the following year, and Packed Home had won the Kerry National in Listowel.

It looked as if Arkle was sauntering to victory when Height O'Fashion, on her featherweight, came after him strongly on the run-in, closing with every stride. In a thrilling spectacle, Arkle found himself in his one and only photo finish – but he held on by a neck.

St Patrick's – Paddy's – Day, 17 March 1966, and Arkle has four rivals for his bid for a third consecutive Cheltenham Gold Cup. He is 1-10 to achieve it, an incredible price given there are also some twenty-two fences to negotiate. But, of course, it is run at level weights – and he had shown himself able to give three stone to good horses and still beat them.

Joe Jones, who now lives in Ashbourne, County Meath, was a student at the East Warwick College of Further Education, Rugby, and was determined to be there.

'There were four of us, Jake Kramer (not the professional American tennis player of the 1940s and 50s) from Australia, Dunstan from Canada, one from the UK and me. We took off the evening before and we slept in the car in Stratford on Avon. It was a Triumph sports car with two seats and a back shelf so we didn't sleep much.

'We arrived at the course so early that we didn't have to pay to get in. We were still well oiled from the previous night! We positioned ourselves near the final fence; I remember Arkle jumping it like a wild stag.

'The next day at college I was singled out for absconding. I was a post-grad, and sponsored by the Electricity Supply Board. Luckily my professor understood Irishmen and said the only thing to do on Paddy's Day was go and see Arkle beat the English-trained horses.'

At Kelly's pub in Ashbourne the bar emptied out when the Gold Cup was about to be run, and the customers crowded into the Kelly family's kitchen where they had a black and white TV.

Peadar Kelly remembers it well – and the party the Duchess threw in the village hall afterwards.

'There were lots of crisps, sweets and minerals for us kids. At the Halloween after his third Gold Cup the Press were taking pictures and we children wore masks all around Arkle, it was on the news. Sean Barker's [one of the Dreapers' lads] kids were tiny and one put her hand up to stroke his belly; it's like it was yesterday.'

Among the crowd that day of Arkle's third Gold Cup was Jim Lewis, now retired, but at the time young and with any future fortune in a furniture-importing business, let alone racehorse owning, no more than a distant dream. He was more interested in Aston Villa Football Club and once he became a racehorse owner he chose the claret and blue strip of the club's 1957 Cup win as his racing colours; apart from Best

Mate's three Gold Cups, he also won the 2000 Queen Mother Champion Chase with Edredon Bleu. But back in 1966, Jim stood on the hill the far side of Cheltenham race-course in the cheap enclosure (now the Best Mate stand) with a group of friends and his wife, Valerie.

'In those days if we had enough money left to buy fish and chips on the way home we'd had a good day.'

Forty years later he was to take tea with the Queen in the Royal Box after one of his three Gold Cup wins with Best Mate.

Deep in County Cork the thirteen-year-old Jonjo O'Neill was hunting his pony, Dolly, with the Duhallow hounds. She had cost £27.2/- from a fair in Tallow a few years earlier; one of the hunt's followers he most admired was Anne, Duchess of Westminster. He remembers her as a very experienced rider who was 'always immaculate whenever she was out hunting.'

She was not there that day, of course, and even the Duhallow hounds, one of Ireland's oldest and most respected hunts, pulled up halfway through the afternoon.

Jonjo O'Neill, former champion jockey who won the memorable Gold Cup with Dawn Run in 1986 and now successful trainer, remembers it distinctly: 'The whole field stopped and went to a small house, they tied the horses and ponies up at the gates and went into this small little cottage that had a black and white TV. The TV had snowflakes running right through the screen like negatives. The race was off and I mainly remember the eleventh fence when Arkle made the most horrendous mistake which stopped him and he went straight through it. The whole cottage was absolutely silent, everyone thought Ireland's chance of winning the Gold Cup was dead; in fact the whole of Ireland's heart stopped for a second. However, through his sheer class, Arkle picked himself up and went on and won very easily.'

That fence is indeed the main memory for most people who watched the race, for the opposition was never going to be a factor. They were

Snaigow 100-7; Dormant, 20-1; Hunch 33-1 and Sartorious 50-1 (opened at 200-1).

It is probably the race, along with his first Gold Cup, that people remember more than any other. Arkle was in a clear lead, enjoying a stroll in the Cotswold air when he appeared to ignore the fence altogether; he seemed about to take off in the correct place, but then didn't, and the next thing was the fence came up to meet him; he breasted it, parting the thick birch. In reflex horseman's action, Pat Taaffe shot his lower legs forward to take the strain and loosened his grip on the reins to allow Arkle to stretch his neck and aid his recovery. It all occurred in a split second. Arkle barely paused in his tracks, but strode on as if nothing had happened, cleared the remaining fences immaculately, including the last fence where he had made that monumental blunder on the previous circuit, and sauntered to a record thirty lengths victory at the record short price of 1-10. Various theories have been put forward as to what caused his blunder (much as they were for Devon Loch's unsolved sprawling on the run-in in the 1956 Grand National when within yards of victory for the Queen Mother). Was it caused by the cheering of the crowds? Did he look at a photographer and 'forget' to jump? Was it simply a momentary lack of concentration? It is interesting listening to Sir Peter O'Sullevan's commentary, because a full fifty yards before the fence he noted that Arkle 'was looking at the crowds'. The blunder certainly wasn't caused by him being pressed by any other horse for he was already a long way clear.

All across Ireland, where friends and strangers alike packed around snowy televisions, right round Great Britain, and every one of the approximately thirty-five thousand racegoers packed into Cheltenham racecourse heaved collective sighs of relief – as did Paddy Woods. He had been put on standby by Tom Dreaper to ride Arkle that day should any mishap befall Pat Taaffe beforehand.

He says magnanimously, 'Pat had long legs, and I don't know that I would have stayed on, I might have gone over his head.'

Eva, Tom Dreaper's daughter, says today, '[Arkle's] survival of that blunder was thanks to the shamrock he was wearing in his bridle!'

CHAPTER 12

LAST RACE –
STUNNED
SILENCE 1966

Allll was set for a crack at Arkle's fourth Gold Cup, and he began
the 1966-67 season later than usual with the Hennessy at Newbury at
the end of November.

Arkle was as well as ever, as he had shown at home one day when he
was set to school alongside Flyingbolt. Pat Taaffe was on Flyingbolt with
Paddy Woods on Arkle. They were to jump a line of four fences, just to
get their eyes in and limber up their 'jumping muscles' for the season
ahead.

It didn't quite go as planned.

Paddy remembers, 'Jesus, we started to go, both horses were flying,
and standing off at the wings; they were taking each other on. Mr
Dreaper was yelling at us to stop, but we couldn't.'

The two horses had been 'eyeballing' each other and made one holy
competition out of it. Luckily nothing untoward happened and Tom
Dreaper laughed – but the two horses never schooled upsides again,

although they did sometimes gallop together.

CRCR

Jockey Stan Mellor walked into the paddock at Newbury, tapping his whip against his polished boot, and doffed his cap to the trainer Ken Cundell and Mr. J.R.J. – Reg – Blundell, owner of a promising young grey called Stalbridge Colonist. He was the 25-1 outsider of the six runners for the 1966 Hennessy Gold Cup, but crucially he had been running in France during the summer. He hadn't been overly impressive, with two falls and a second placing, but he was race-fit; it was Arkle's first run of the season and Stan Mellor had a plan.

'My horse had a blinding bit of speed and I fancied my chances.'

Son of a Manchester builder, Stan Mellor first sat on a pony at the age of nine, and won a jumping competition just two weeks later. He became an apprentice to George Owen, a renowned jockey mentor of future champions, and Stan, in his turn, was champion three times and became the first English jockey to ride a thousand National Hunt winners. Apart from riding ability, Stan Mellor also possessed a racing brain. He was to put it to effective use this day.

Thirty-three miles away at Eton, sixteen-year-old Nicky Henderson was in cahoots with one of his tutors, racing fan Michael Kidson.

'It was coming up to St Andrew's Day and we were meant to be watching some silly football match; we sloped off [to Newbury] in his Morris Minor, so he was also taking a risk.'

The pair couldn't go into the members' enclosure because Nicky's father, Johnny Henderson, was a steward, so they opted for the safety of the last fence, away from prying eyes – they thought. To be caught at a race-meeting would 'be second only to murder in terms of the worst crime.'

Back in the paddock, trainer Ken Cundell was trying to curb Stan Mellor's enthusiasm for his own hopes; he thought he had a chance of winning.

'He was not very pleased with me and tried to shush me up,' Stan recalls, 'because he had been trying to explain to the owner how good Arkle was, and he didn't want him to be disappointed. The owner was new to racing and as chairman of Plymouth Argyle Football Club he could only understand win or lose. The next year, when Stalbridge Colonist was second in the Cheltenham Gold Cup, he didn't come to the unsaddling enclosure.'

Ken Cundell gave his orders to his jockey, and added that if he was not happy with the horse he should pull him up on the far side.

Arkle had his customary 12 stone 7lbs, What A Myth carried 10 stone 2lbs, Freddie was on 10 stone 7lbs due to a 7lb penalty, and Stalbridge Colonist, Kellsboro' Wood and Master Mascus were on 10 stone.

Nine-year-old Sean Bell, now a Curragh farrier, remembers that his father, Paddy, a brother-in-law to Ken Cundall's head man Billy Carroll, had been advised to back Stalbridge Colonist in a forecast to come second to Arkle at a price of 14-1. He was unable to watch the race on television because the family did not acquire one until the following year.

CƷCR

Stan Mellor takes up the story. 'There was no horse to make the running so Arkle had to. I could see the race might suit me if I didn't threaten Arkle; I was running up his backside into the last fence so when Pat looked round he didn't see me. When he faced back, I hoicked Stalbridge Colonist out. He veered right and wide and Arkle didn't know

I was there. My aim was to get to the last fence during his one spell of speed and stay on. We went flat out into the last and landed running.'

By the time Stalbridge Colonist had edged ahead there wasn't enough time left for Arkle to rally; the post came too soon and the young whippersnapper, in receipt of 2 ½ stone, won by half a length.

Stan remains adamant that Pat Taaffe did nothing wrong, and also insists it wasn't the weight that beat Arkle, but the rapier bit of speed from Stalbridge Colonist at the one required moment.

'Anyway, it worked.'

But surely if Stalbridge Colonist had carried the same weight as Arkle he would not have won?

'That's true, he wouldn't.'

So it was a combination of weight and crafty, cunning jockeyship. Has he ever regretted beating the great horse?

'Sorry to beat him? Never!'

Eddie Harty didn't have a ride in the race and reckoned he knew what his contemporary Stan Mellor might do.

'My father taught me to wait and wait and wait, you can only beat them once and that needs to be at the winning line, not a fence before or a stride after.'

He used to undertake cash betting for Gay Kindersley and backed the grey for him on this occasion, a nice pay day.

Eddie Harty says, 'Arkle failed by half a length to give 35lbs to Stalbridge Colonist. The merit of that performance should be gauged by the fact that the winner went on to be placed twice in future Cheltenham Gold Cups and the third horse, What A Myth, won the Gold Cup in 1969.'

For Paddy Bell, the forecast was the wrong way round and so there was no dividend for him.

Nicky Henderson and Michael Kidson were at the last fence and couldn't see the finish.

'Then we heard Arkle was beaten,' Nicky says. 'He was the absolute legend; I had a picture of Mill House and Arkle in my room at school instead of a pin-up, sad really! Arkle was the only horse who could ever get his picture on the front page of the *Sunday Times*, any others were sports pages only which the headmaster would never look at; and there it was next day, the last fence with us watching and the head saw it. We were summoned to him, it was the only time I met him in my entire school life there; I think we got off by calling it "education".'

Not so lucky was Ireland's future champion trainer, Noel Meade, on another occasion that Arkle was running. Noel was boarding at an agricultural college at Multyfarnham, near Mullingar when he feigned sickness; his idea was to skip lessons and get out to one of the few televisions to watch the race. Instead the priest, suspecting exactly what his pupil was up to, sent him to his dormitory and locked the door!

When Queen Anne paid £558 19/5d for Ascot Heath in 1711 it was strictly for Flat racing, and began with her Queen's Plate in July of that year, ('steeple-chasing' or racing from 'point to point' was 'invented' in 1752 in Ireland with a famous match between two hunters from Buttevant to Doneraile in County Cork).

One of the most traditional places on earth, it was not until 1965 that 'jump racing' finally came to Ascot, and so it was only in its second year when Arkle contested the 1966 SGB Handicap Chase two-and-a-half weeks after the Hennessy. No one that December day could have predicted they were to see Arkle win for the last time. It is all the more special in that it was one of his really easy victories.

Johnny Lumley recalls, 'Arkle was getting very excited before his races by this time, so it was decided to leave him unplaited to keep him calmer. It seemed to work – and he won as he normally did, picking up where he had left off before the Hennessy.'

There were four other horses in the race, Sunny Bright, Vultrix, Big George and Master Mascus, but they were barely supporting players, more bit parts. Arkle put in a superb round of jumping, galloping from fence to fence. The others remained a deferential distance behind, occasionally trying to join him only to be brushed aside, and this time there was no surprise lurking in the wings. Arkle was never headed, and although the ground was heavy, and he jumped slightly left-handed over the last few fences, he drew away to win imperiously by fifteen lengths, once more the undisputed master of all he surveyed. After his battles against inferior horses when carrying crucifying weights, he deserved it. That day he epitomised everything he represented and we remember him for.

Richard Pitman was on the runner up, Sunny Bright. He remembers, 'The most noticeable things about him were how lean, easy moving and greyhound looking he was. He was always travelling easily yet once we made any inroads towards challenging, he simply went up a gear to leave us like we were running through treacle whereas he was floating on air. My horse never reproduced his old form, Arkle seemed to demoralise him.'

And yet, and yet ... there was some unease in the Arkle camp. Himself was thoroughly checked over, but nothing amiss was found. Pat Taaffe recalls in his memoir that his action had been slightly off-key and he sensed there was something wrong.

Nevertheless the ease of his win boded well for Arkle's fourth Gold Cup in March 1967.

Before then, he would run in the King George VI on Boxing Day and take in a home prep race, probably Leopardstown again, before returning to Cheltenham. That was the plan.

CB CB

Frost caused a twenty-four-hour postponement of Kempton's Christmas feature and a pulled muscle resulted in the withdrawal of Mill House. Tom Dreaper's daughter, Eva, was stuck at home, looking after him – 'not the sort of thing a teenager wants to do, I wanted to be out.'

Sean Bell was in bed with flu, and there was no television in the house. Neither was there in Leopardstown where Irish crowds flocked for part of their Christmas Festival.

The frost had given way to gloom rather than bright sunshine, but Arkle would soon sparkle for the sixteen thousand spectators at Kempton Park, of that they were sure. His opponents were Woodland Venture (winner of his previous two races and who was to win the next Gold Cup), Dormant, who had been second to Arkle by a distance in the previous year's King George and by thirty lengths in the Gold Cup; Maigret, winner of three chases; the Duchess's former horse Foinavon; Scottish Final and Arctic Ocean.

The crowds anticipated an exhibition round from Himself. It was not to be. Probably as early as the second fence Arkle's front foot rapped the take-off board and broke his pedal bone. With the benefit of hindsight, it is not surprising he did not run with his usual authority; the *élan* was not there, nor the jumping dash and he barely pulled at Pat Taaffe's arms at all. In the heat of the race, of course, the adrenalin kept flowing, so neither horse nor rider realised something was wrong. But two out, Woodland Venture looked ominous, only to fall.

The way was left clear for Arkle and as he led over the last those who loved him – everyone – drew in collective breaths; they began cheering him home up the run in. Dormant was a mere speck behind him, albeit that he was closing. And closing some more. Arkle, at nine years old and in his prime – this was not a handicap, remember, and he wasn't giving away stones to his rivals – was slowing. Dormant came on some more. Was the unthinkable about to happen? Surely not. The indomitable Arkle is flagging. He never flags, never, not even when faced with a lightweight snapping at his heels. But now he can barely raise a gallop. Dormant has gone by him. The crowd's cheers turn to groans. Dormant by a length. Dormant! Silence descends into the gloom. And then they see it. As Arkle pulls up to walk in, he is lame.

Ironically, the Number One single in the charts that day was Tom Jones' 'The Green, Green Grass of Home'. No one could have foretold it, but that was where Arkle was headed.

Over in Ireland, the Leopardstown Christmas Festival was in full flow. A number of spectators may have had radios to listen to Arkle's race. By whatever means, the news got out somehow that Arkle had been beaten.

Robert Hall, now an RTÉ racing presenter, was pestering his father, Goff's Sales manager Michael, but all he remembers is his agitation and consternation as the news filtered through.

'But no-one knew what had happened,' Robert remembers.

Back at Kempton, Captain Ryan Price, who had been a Commando in WWII, took administrative control; firstly, he held the crowds at bay, and later he arranged with Betty Dreaper for a roster of his own lads to come to Kempton from Findon in Sussex to help look after Arkle, at least until Betty had a chance to organise a relay of lads, a week at a time, from Ireland.

That's the sort of man Captain Price was. The following year, Ryan Price was to face a career-threatening crisis of his own when his Schweppes (now Tote) handicap hurdle winner Hill House was deemed to have been doped. Eventually, after lengthy testing thanks to one of his owners, Lady Weir (whose What A Myth was to win the 1969 Gold Cup), it was proved beyond doubt that Hill House manufactured his own 'non normal nutrient' cortisol, and Ryan Price was exonerated.

Back in the unsaddling enclosure at Kempton it was hoped at first that Arkle had done no more than hit a nerve. A farrier arrived and took the shoe off Arkle's sore foot. Paddy Woods gave a nail from it to a spectator. People were still crushing round, craning their necks, the winner long since gone back to the stables to be washed down. Paddy kept the shoe for about a year, until the Duchess asked for it as she wanted to get it mounted. (When she died, she left Paddy a silver fruit salver inscribed 'To the Duchess of Westminster in recognition of her part in the combined achievements of Arkle, Tom Dreaper and Pat Taaffe Presented by the Anglo American Sporting Club.')

Arkle was put into a trailer and driven down to the racecourse stables.

Vet Maxie Cosgrove flew over the next day. Groom Johnny Lumley, of course, was already there. Still relatively naive, he asked Maxie if Arkle would be able to run in the Gold Cup, two and a half months away.

'I didn't realise how serious it was, that the end was staring me in the face. The injury was devastating, we had been looking at six Gold Cups and the chance was gone.'

Johnny was flown home the following day, and then returned for Arkle's last seven days of six weeks in plaster, so that he could travel home with his superstar. Regular bulletins appeared in the press and on television and radio. Get-well cards and letters adorned his box. Such was his celebrity that an address was unnecessary; a number of cards and letters simply addressed 'Arkle, Ireland' found their way to his box. One was addressed 'Arkle, Ireland, near London'! It still reached him.

When it was time to go home, throngs of well-wishers and TV crews saw him off from Birmingham airport, and even more greeted his arrival at Dublin. And as ever, Johnny Lumley's face stared out of the next day's newspapers, but readers were looking at Arkle not the young man with the curly mop of nearly black hair.

'Oh, yes, Arkle was up there with the Beatles and Muhammad Ali,' he remembers proudly. 'But it was great for me, too, in spite of the discomfort of flying with horses.'

He explains, 'It was the early days of flying horses and the planes were adapted cargo vessels; they were quite dangerous, and very cold. The stalls were rough and ready with sharp edges, and people used to go around looking for a ramp to bring the horses down when we landed.

'It was freezing cold and we couldn't talk because it was so noisy, so we used to sit on a bale of straw and play cards. The journey from Dublin to Birmingham took two and a half hours.'

Recuperation for Arkle continued first at Greenogue and in time at Bryanstown, once it was safe to turn him out to grass. Later there would be the come-back trail.

But ultimately, it was to the 'Green, Green Grass of Home' that Arkle was headed.

CHAPTER 13

STEALING THE SHOW

T hat Arkle came within a few days of running again would not have been the case had Tom Dreaper been well, his elder daughter, Eva, believes.

'If my father had been in good health I don't think he would have entertained it; he was a strongly opinionated man, but I think the fight had gone out of him to argue. I remember Arkle coming back in September, but he was weak, his coat was dull and his eye wasn't bright.'

He spent that winter of 1967-68 in Greenogue, and finally, in April, he was due to run in a two and a half mile hurdle race at nearby Fairyhouse at the Easter Festival where a new race had been especially framed for him. A few days before it, Pat Taaffe schooled him; Pat did not feel the old fire-power there, and he told Tom Dreaper. The Duchess was consulted, too, of course, and the much-heralded come-back was postponed. Perhaps he would reappear at the Leopardstown Christmas Festival at the end of the year. So Arkle returned to Bryanstown for another summer at grass – interspersed with many visitors – but in October, rather than return him to training at rising twelve years old, his retirement was announced.

The Duchess said, 'Arkle is sound and very well … After a great deal of thought and discussions with Tom Dreaper and Mr Cosgrove, we have decided to retire him. Not even Arkle, with his immense courage, could be expected to reproduce his old brilliance.'

Wisdom from the people around the great horse had, as ever, prevailed.

Arkle remained a star, and probably the highlight of his all-too-brief retirement was his visit to the Horse of the Year Show at Wembley in October 1969, where he concluded the parade of horse personalities each evening, ridden by Pat Taaffe or with Paddy Woods deputising.

Johnny Lumley had by this time left Greenogue (firstly to work in a pub in England and then to work for Eircom in Ireland) but Paddy Woods recalls the week in London.

'It was a great week. Arkle was stabled about half an hour away on a big estate; I can't remember what it was called. He seemed as well as ever. The Duchess came over two mornings, and I ran him up for her in a headcollar.

'In the nightly parade at the show there was a well-known apple and orange man with a donkey and cart. Arkle loved sweets; he could smell them in a pocket from three yards away. On the last night we decided to have a bit of craic. A tune was played for every horse, and for Arkle it was "There'll never be another you." The cart man stopped in front of me, and I let Arkle look at it, I let the reins loose and he nosed the back of the cart, and started scoffing like a child. He ate a big hamper of fruit and he got huge applause, it brought the house down.'

Above: Queen Elizabeth, the Queen Mother, presents Anne, Duchess of Westminster with the Cheltenham Gold Cup.

Right: Arkle parading at the Dublin show and looking superb.

Left and below: Stable lad Johnny Lumley had a particular rapport with 'his' horse, Arkle.

Above: Arkle stretching his legs at home in Bryanstown, County Kildare, in 1966.

Right: Inquisitive – the Duchess on Arkle at Eaton Lodge.

Above: The Duchess and Arkle.

Below: Hellen Egan (right), Dr Michael Osborne of the Irish National Stud (centre) and a colleague work on Arkle's skeleton.

Above: Arkle's skeleton on display at the National Stud.

Below: The Queen's visit to the National Stud, 19 May 2011. Left to right: Jim Dreaper, Alison Baker (red jacket), Willie Robinson, TP Burns and Paddy Woods. (Maxwell Photography)

Above: Ted Walsh (left) and Robert Hall (centre) RTE television presenters, Leopardstown.

Below: Stan Mellor, who in a canny ride beat Arkle on Stalbridge Colonist, in front of the statue of Dawn Run.

Above: Alison Baker at home in 2013, holding the catalogue for Arkle's sale.

Right: Pat Taaffe's grandsons, Pat (left) & Alex, at their father Tom Taaffe's home.

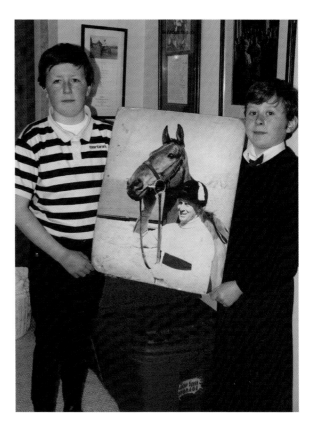

Above: Paddy Woods in the foundry with the almost finished statue of Arkle and Pat Taaffe.

Below: TP Burns today; he rode Arkle to win his only Flat race.

Arkle remained in demand although for the most part it was a life of pampered luxury in the paddocks of Bryanstown, under the watchful eye of Johnny Kelly, and turned out with Meg, the Duchess's grey hunter. They became devoted companions. Arkle's lazy days at Bryanstown were frequently peppered by visitors, some by appointment including famous film stars, sculptors and artists, and others who turned up on the doorstep. Such casual visitors wanting to visit and pat Arkle were indulged, like Michael and Margaret Murray who named their Yorkshire home Arkle House. Originally from Mullingar, Michael says, 'I went to see Arkle with my wife Margaret; we called at Kilcock Garda station and asked for directions. We went in to Bryanstown and two guys in the yard said, "Have you come to see the horse?" Arkle was being got ready for the Horse of the Year Show, and we were allowed to take photographs. A boy led Arkle into the paddock, he stood majestically with his head in the air, he knew who he was.'

Another visitor was Will Reilly whose father, Tom Reilly, from Dunboyne, worked as a blacksmith for Tom Dreaper; his brother, James (Will's uncle), cared for Arkle's feet during his retirement.

'Mr Dreaper wrote my father a lovely testimonial.'

Will Reilly wrote an article about his childhood hero in a blog post on Boylesports.com in March 2012.

He recalled, 'As a young lad, I had the enormous good fortune to meet Arkle. He was in retirement in County Kildare and a cousin of mine – my family hails from a long line of blacksmiths – was involved with his welfare.

'I have a picture to mark the occasion: Arkle with one of my sisters plus our cousin. It must have been the early seventies given her bright, floral dress and Dame Edna glasses. She has a smile in the picture as wide as the winning distance of Arkle's third Gold Cup. And why not? She had just met, stroked, fed and patted one of racing's greatest legends, had got a hair from his tail and even a lick of her autograph book from him. We still have the hair and the book and, of course, the memories.

'Things that you remember about Arkle are his confidence, gentleness and presence. Ok, I was a small being at the time, but I still felt that I was in the company of something special. He gently walked over when he saw us and took great interest, in a gentle way, of all that was going on.

'There was no nastiness or intrusion to him and he held his head high and inquisitively in a manner that suggested a confidence and love of life.

'My father, who once worked for Arkle's trainer Tom Dreaper, had backed Arkle for the 1963 Hennessy Gold Cup at Newbury. You see, he had met up with Mr Dreaper at Newbury and, in his masterfully understated way, [Mr Dreaper] had told Dad that it was quite possible that Arkle was a bit better than Prince Regent.

'Yes, that's the Prince Regent who, in 1946, won the Champion Chase and Gold Cup at Cheltenham – and that was when his career was in decline, the Second World War having denied him the chance to be tested in his prime.

'You can understand, then, why Dad backed Arkle. However, Arkle got beaten in the Hennessy, an uncharacteristic mistake early in the home straight putting paid to his chances on a foggy day in Berkshire. The race was won by Mill House, the rising star of English chasing that had landed the 1963 Cheltenham Gold Cup as a mere six-year-old.

'No other six-year-old had won the Gold Cup since Mill House until Long Run galloped to victory in 2011. In fact, Mill House had been the only six-year-old in fifty years to win staying chasing's blue riband event until Long Run came along.

'Undeterred – for Tom Dreaper's greatness was heavily backed up by astuteness – Dad headed for Cheltenham and the 1964 Gold Cup. He cut a fairly lonely figure in the "Arkle queue" as the gang who had derided him for backing Arkle at Newbury, looked to play up their Mill

House winnings.

'Well, the rest, as they say is history. Arkle galloped up the Cheltenham hill to inflict a defeat on Fulke Walwyn's hugely-talented gelding from which, some said, he never recovered.

'His brilliance established, Arkle went on to confirm his greatness by winning the Gold Cup again in 1965 and 1966 and he remains the benchmark against which chasers are measured ...

'By this time, Anne, Duchess of Westminster's gelding had become a household name and was immovably etched into racing's psyche and folklore, particularly in Ireland, although his fame and reputation extended far beyond the Emerald Isle.'

Arkle even had a song written and recorded on 45rpm vinyl about him. Entitled simply 'Arkle', it was written by Dominic Behan.

Eva says, 'I have a copy, it will be something for my grandchildren. It still gets air time on radio stations come Cheltenham time.'

CHAPTER 14

'ARKLE IS DEAD'

On Sunday 31 May 1970, Valerie Dreaper, younger daughter of Arkle's trainer Tom, was in the school san at Bedgebury Park, Kent, not the most salubrious of places at the best of times, suffering from pre-exam nerves.

'I hadn't done any revision for my O-levels, and I suddenly realised my parents had spent all that money on my education.'

So Valerie was unwell, but unbeknownst to her, so was Arkle.

About a hundred kilometres away from Valerie's boarding school, Paddy Woods and his wife Phyllis were enjoying a holiday in the London area for the Epsom Derby the following Wednesday, June 3. One of the first things Paddy did was visit Kempton Park and renew acquaintanceship with friends he had made when looking after Arkle during the weeks of veterinary care.

The couple had an enjoyable time there, followed by lunch in Sunbury, close to the River Thames. As they walked along the pavement afterwards there was a newspaper seller.

Paddy stopped in his tracks as he read the headline blazing out at him.

He knew nothing of what had happened so unexpectedly back in Ireland just after he had left for his holiday and neither, of course, did

Valerie as she lay in her sick bed.

For back in Bryanstown Pat Taaffe had called in to visit his old pal with his daughter, Olive, eldest of his four children; Arkle recognised him and looked at him with his enquiring eye; Pat gave him an apple and fussed over him, but then as he went to close the door, he wrote in *My Life and Arkle's*, 'I had to move him back a foot and when I did he almost fell. I realised once again that it was only courage and pride now keeping him on his feet …'

Arthritis in his hind feet had been plaguing him for some time, but he wasn't responding to treatment. As soon as he could reach a phone Pat called both the vet, Maxie Cosgrove, and the Duchess herself. He urged her to fly over at once.

That afternoon some of the principal players in Arkle's life conferred. For Olive Taaffe, who was a young child, the day he died remains her only clear Arkle memory: the huddle of adults discussing what to do about the great horse, who, she remembers, 'was obviously in pain'.

The only sane decision was reached. One of Maxie Cosgrove's partners in Riversdale Clinic, Lucan, James Kavanagh (the other partner was Seán Collins) walked to the back of the car and filled the syringe. The mighty Arkle would have felt nothing beyond the prick of what could have been a routine injection. It was not, and the greatest steeplechaser the world has ever known passed peacefully away. He was only thirteen years old.

Valerie heard the news on her bedside radio.

Paddy Woods stood rooted to the pavement, staring in disbelief at the headline on the front page of the newspaper, *'Arkle is Dead'*.

Three days later Nijinsky, one of the greatest Irish Flat racehorses and future champion stallion, ran away with the Derby. I wonder if Arkle was looking down and cheering 'At-a-boy!'

CRCR

It was Eva who issued the statement to the Press. Arkle was buried at Bryanstown, joined not all that long afterwards by his long time companion, Meg. A little hedge, kept neatly clipped, was planted round the two inscribed grave stones.

Tributes and letters of condolence poured in. Betty Dreaper and Mrs Tinsley coped with those that arrived by the sackful at Greenogue. Anne, Duchess of Westminster, replied to those that came to her, including one from Christina Veal, whose father, Bill, had died the year before.

> Dear Christina,
>
> Thank you so very, very much for writing to me. I know how sorry you all will feel. I really have lost one of my dearest friends, he was such a <u>pet</u> and I'm afraid I'll always think of him as that more than the most wonderful race horse in the world. Please give my love to your mother.
>
> Yours ever,
>
> Anne Westminster

CRCR

In 1976, Anne, Duchess of Westminster moved out of Bryanstown and into nearby Derrinstown.

It severed a strong link with her late husband and was a big wrench, as was selling her prize Jersey herd, which was no longer paying its way. Bryanstown had been bought by the Duke along with the adjacent Derrinstown back in the 1940s soon after the purchase of Fort William – the home where Nancy scandalously spent the night at the start of her love affair with the Duke.

There became a fear that Bryanstown might be built over after the Duchess sold it – not so, as it happens, because in the early 1980s it became part of the deputy ruler of Dubai, Sheikh Hamdan bin Rashid Al Maktoum's magnificent Derrinstown Stud, which he also bought, the 375 acres having since expanded to two thousand.

The planned new museum at the Irish National Stud was looking for a centrepiece attraction. Who better than Arkle? A request was made by the stud manager, Michael Osborne, to the Duchess, the idea being, according to the book *Nancy*, 'so that the amazingly capacious rib cage which had been responsible in part for his remarkable performances could by studied by students of both racing and equine physiology.'

Rather than risk Arkle's grave being ignominiously buried beneath new houses, the Duchess reluctantly agreed to donate his skeleton. Today the museum, along with the Irish National Stud and its Japanese Gardens, is one of Ireland's leading visitor attractions. The digging up of Arkle's skeleton was certainly controversial, and for those most closely associated with Himself it was hurtful.

Paddy Woods says, 'I was a bit shocked when Arkle was dug up but the Duchess had sold the land and it could have become a housing estate. Pat Taaffe was not in favour, either.'

For others, it is something to show their children. Penny Prendergast, second of Kevin Prendergast's seven daughters born the year Arkle first ran, 1961, took her three daughters to the Irish National Stud to see the skeleton; Kevin rode the winner of Arkle's second ever race at Leopardstown.

'Arkle was like a myth, a legend, and so much a part of Irish life and racing.'

Breeder's daughter Alison Baker abhorred the thought of Arkle's remains being dug up, and she only accepted the invitation to meet the Queen at the Irish National Stud in May 2011 on condition that she would not have to see the skeleton.

She says, 'I talked to the Queen about the Duchess and how she loved all her horses; she then moved on to Paddy Woods – and he talked to her non-stop!'

Paddy recalls, 'I couldn't believe it when I got the invite, I got some stick from friends.'

Lady O'Reilly and John Osborne, chairperson and chief executive respectively of the Irish National Stud, accompanied the Queen when the stallions paraded. Trainer Jessie Harrington, a Stud director, introduced the Queen to fellow Irish trainers, including Willie Mullins, Paul Nolan and Mouse Morris; and jockey Johnny Murtagh introduced her to the RACE (Racing Academy and Centre of Education) students, where Prince Philip the Duke of Edinburgh took an interest in the galloping racehorse simulator. Finally, Jim Dreaper was her guide in the Museum. Also associated with Arkle and among those invited that day, along with Jim Dreaper, Paddy Woods and Alison Baker, were Jim's wife, Patricia, Willie Robinson (rider of Mill House), TP Burns (rider of Arkle in his only Flat race), Peter Reynolds of Ballymacoll Stud where Arkle was born, Olive Taaffe, and a nephew of Alison Baker.

Peter Reynolds, current manager of Ballymacoll Stud, says, 'When we were down to meet the Queen on her Irish National Stud visit, she said to me "What's a flat breeder like you doing among all the Arkle people? So I told her the story."'

Alison Baker, who had just turned ninety-one, achieved her aim of not seeing Arkle's skeleton, and was in good health on that spring day.

The person charged with piecing Arkle together again was Sally Carroll from the Irish National Stud, under the project manager, Mary McGrath.

Mary McGrath remembers it as being a bit contentious at the time, but also that his skeleton became an asset to the stud's students.

'There were huge numbers interested in seeing it, and it was a very good teaching aid. His skeleton shows how deep his heart room was. There was a girl in London at the time called Chesty Morgan of whom it was said her bust was bigger than Arkle's!'

Mary remembers hunting through Bryanstown 'and all the men took their hats off to Arkle as we passed by his grave.

'He was an incredible horse, and his skeleton was ideal to be the centrepiece of the new museum.'

Award winning racing writer Lissa Oliver interviewed Sally Carroll for an Australian magazine called *Racetrack* in 2006 and told the story.

… Sally was responsible for the stud's brightest star, the jewel in the crown that attracts thousands of visitors to the Stud's Museum each year – Arkle. Or more correctly, of course, his skeleton. It was Sally who not only assembled the famed artefact, but physically unearthed the bones of this great racing legend.

You might wonder how one gets from the relative normality of office and admin to wielding a shovel in an orchard on Derrinstown Stud, is it a matter of being in the right – or possibly the wrong! – place at the right time? Sally laughs ruefully.

'Looking back it was an honour to do it, and I feel very proud to be associated with it,' she says. The late Michael Osborne, stud manager, had always wanted to create a museum of racing and when the opportunity arose he knew he needed something very special to pull in the crowds. There was nothing more special than Arkle, the magic of his name still as strong today as it was at the height of his illustrious career during the mid 1960s.

Sally, an Australian student called Hellen Egan and a lad by the name of Steve, descended on the small orchard at Bryanstown armed with shovels. There, in 1976, six years after his death, they unearthed Arkle from the plot that he shared with Meg. Meg's grave was left untouched.

Sally admits that the work was pretty gory stuff. Many of the bones were still covered in hair and flesh, but they were popped in a wheelbarrow and eventually into the back of a jeep to fetch back to the stud. There was no question of putting them in any kind of order.

'I soaked them in bins filled with a cleaning solution which probably wasn't the right thing to do, but the stench was vile,' Sally remembers. 'The museum was still under construction, and it had a large flat roof with just a gentle slope. I needed somewhere to dry the bones so we laid them out all over the roof! I remember arriving one morning and seeing the building covered in birds. I was so afraid they would carry off all the bones!'

But there was no such luck for Sally! It was later her job, together with Hellen Egan, to assemble the bones, though they had no veterinary experience between them!

'Michael [Osborne] gave us a veterinary book with photos in it and assured us it would be as simple as doing a jigsaw!' Sally recalls. 'We did a fair bit of rummaging and occasionally Michael would find a correct piece for us, but really it did fit together quite well. If the pieces belonged, they fitted easily. It was rather like doing one of those 3D jigsaw puzzles.'

Just like a jigsaw puzzle, there was inevitably a piece missing. 'The very smallest bone, from the tip of the tail, went missing. It was probably taken by someone, as a souvenir. It was the trend in America at the time to have the tooth of a favourite horse plated in gold or silver and mounted on a necklace. That's probably what happened to that one tiny bone.'

Sally is quite indignant about such manhandling and lack of honour shown to Arkle, but as always it's with good humour. 'Arkle wasn't protected by a case and visitors always touched him, which worried me in terms of care, but also I felt it was very disrespectful! I was showing a friend round the museum one day and I happened to be ranting about the lack of respect and the way people constantly prodded and poked him. I reached over and pointed out the place where the missing bone was and as I touched the base of the tail the whole tail fell off! I was horrified! All the visitors turned round to see what had happened and gave me the most shocking looks!'

Fortunately there was no better person to hand than Sally herself – the tail bones were quickly re-assembled! Needless to say, that wasn't the only embarrassing incident the Bones of Arkle have been responsible for.

'When the Museum was opened the Duchess of Westminster was invited to see Arkle's exhibit, for the first time. Naturally it was a very poignant moment for her, it was actually very sad. She said that she would have preferred to just remember him as he was.' But she very nearly had cause to remember him just a little too well. 'That morning the lads, who were always up to devilment and pulling pranks, left some hay by his forefeet and a little pile of droppings under his tail! Luckily we got it cleared away just in time!'

For Hellen Egan, who today is a Parts Inventory Analyst for Hastings Deering (Australia) Ltd, it was an amazing experience and opportunity. She says,

We had no experience and it was all guesswork and gut feeling, then seeing what fitted. The most difficult were the knees with all the little bones. I remember Michael [Osborne] giving us a book and I eventually nutted it out, that was a great win for me. It is always a memory that stays with me. The few people I have told I'm sure they don't believe me. Even when I look back I think that was such a huge task but we did it as if it was just another day in our lives.

Sally mentioned the tail bones were missing. I'm not sure from that, if she thought they were taken after we brought him up or before he was buried. But from my recollection I always thought they were never buried with him. I know we searched for them and I always remember the two last tail bones and the feet were missing. From what I remember being told, the owner had the feet made into ashtrays, which in those days was not unusual, but today sounds 'bloody awful'.

For me being Australian, I knew he was important, but I don't think I really realised just how important he was.

When we initially assembled the spine on the metal rod, both Sally and I pretended to be riding a race on it, funny but disrespectful in hindsight.

According to the Duchess's biographer, Robin Rhoderick-Jones, in *Nancy*, 'she hated the final result, while quite understanding the advantages to veterinary science.'

CHAPTER 15

MEMORABILIA

Nick O'Toole grew up at Stepaside, a couple of miles from Leopardstown, 'real racing country,' and surrounded by roads such as Arkle Square, The Gallops and Orby Avenue. The reason was that the developments had been built on the estate of Joe McGrath and his sons, Paddy, Seamus and Joseph of Glencairn House; Joe McGrath was not only one of Ireland's top trainers but he is even better remembered as the inventor of the Irish Hospital Sweeps which sponsored, and thereby transformed, the Irish Derby. It was said he 'employed half the parish'. Flat jockeys Pat Eddery and his father Jimmy both began their careers there, and another incumbent was Australian Bill Williamson.

'They had the best gallops in the world,' Nick O'Toole remembers, 'but the whole area is now built over, a part of prosperous South County Dublin.'

Leopardstown, not surprisingly, was the first race meeting Nick O'Toole ever attended but it was more than that: Arkle was to run, and Nick's father, James, recognising that Arkle was a superstar, wanted his nine-year-old son to see him in the flesh. It was the 1966 Leopardstown Chase.

'It remains a vivid memory,' Nick says, 'and I held on to the race-card.'

From then on, Nick began collecting items about Arkle, from newspaper cuttings to the saddle bought at auction that Pat Taaffe had used on him. Nick O'Toole does not keep all the memorabilia for himself; he acquires it to share (and to turn a penny on), believing that the tangible memorabilia of Arkle should be open to the public to see and enjoy and wonder.

He sold the bulk of his collection to Derek Carruthers of Foley's Antiques in Naas, Co Kildare where it is on display, but it also goes on tour a few times a year to places like the Punchestown NH Festival. Various further pieces of memorabilia have gone to a number of pubs and hotels. Fan letters and get well cards remain popular at many locations.

He says, 'The English really took to Arkle, most of the fan mail came from England. Golden Miller and Cottage Rake's races were not broadcast and so Arkle was the first to really appeal to the masses.'

During the fiftieth anniversary year of the start of Arkle's career special Arkle days were held at Dundalk, Naas and Bellewstown, with commemorative racecards produced and the Arkle collection put on display. Lester Piggott came to Bellewstown in August 2011.

Nick O'Toole says, 'It was two legends and added to the sense of occasion. Lester loved it.'

Nick O'Toole has also made a film using colour footage from the Duchess's private archive. He has Neil Tobin narrating it and music by The Chieftains, a traditional Irish music group. The film shows nine of Arkle's races including his three Gold Cups.

'I interviewed the Duchess at Eaton Lodge, and she was very gracious and charming, she loved the horse so much; she treated us royally for the film. The intention was to show Arkle from the people's point of view, and to be there for posterity.'

In 2010 Nick heard on the grapevine that one of the two saddles used by Pat Taaffe on Arkle was being auctioned by Sotheby's/Graham Budd in London that November. It had first been auctioned for charity in 1970 by Pat Taaffe, who sold it for about £150. The buyer had it for thirty-nine years, until he died, when the daughter discovered it while going through her father's effects, and she put it up for auction.

Nick remembers, 'Pat had two saddles, one light, one heavier, and I checked thoroughly that it was the genuine article for sale by using photos and so on.

'I wanted the saddle to come back to Ireland; I felt it was part of our heritage.'

The hammer price was £11,000 with commission on top of that; a sum Nick O'Toole feels was good value.

'Arkle got to the general populace; watching him live helped to create the legend.

'The problem with memorabilia is you can get selfish with it and keep it at home and nobody can see it; equally, if I part with any of it I'm particular about where it goes.'

Two years later one of Arkle's bridles came up for sale in the same auction. It had been sold in a charity auction in 1970 to raise funds for the Arkle statue at Cheltenham racecourse for £150. This time round it fetched £8,800.

LOT 642 THE ARKLE SADDLE

The saddle used by Pat Taaffe for all of Arkle's victories, set with a metal plaque inscribed 'THIS IS THE SADDLE I USED WHEN I RODE "ARKLE" TO WIN ALL HIS RACES', then engraved with the signature of Pat Taaffe; sold with a typescript letter, undated but circa 1970, signed by Neil Durden-Smith, then Secretary of the Anglo-American Sporting Club, on Club letterhead, reading 'TO WHOM IT MAY CONCERN, THIS IS TO AUTHENTICATE THAT ARKLE'S SADDLE, SIGNED BY PAT TAAFFE, AND NOW OWNED BY MR. ARTHUR POWNALL, IS TRULY THE SADDLE USED

DURING ALL OF ARKLE'S GREAT VICTORIES', the letter sent in response to a request from Arthur Pownall who had purchased the saddle at an Anglo-American Sporting Club after dinner auction (2)

Arkle is universally regarded as being the greatest steeplechaser of all time. His Timeform rating of 212 has never been eclipsed. In recent times Kauto Star has come closest, with a Timeform rating of 191.

The gelding was bred by Mary Baker at the Ballymacoll Stud, owned by Anne, Duchess of Westminster, trained by Tom Dreaper at Greenogue, Kilsallaghan, Co. Dublin, and ridden by Pat Taaffe. Arkle won a total of 27 victories from 35 races and was the first steeplechaser to capture the imagination of the public including those in general with little or no interest in horse racing.

Arkle won three consecutive Cheltenham Gold Cups between 1964 and 1966, whilst other major victories included the King George VI Chase (1965), the Irish Grand National (1964), two Hennessy Gold Cups (1964 & 1965), three Leopardstown Chases (1964-1966 inc.), a Whitbread Gold Cup (1965), the Gallagher Gold Cup (1965), the Punchestown Gold Cup (1963) and the Powers Gold Cup (1963). There would almost certainly have been more, but for a career ending injury sustained in the 1966 King George.

In Ireland Arkle gained legendary status and received fan mail within envelopes simply addressed 'Himself, Ireland'. His commemorations include a statue at Cheltenham Racecourse, who also host the Arkle Challenge Trophy at the Festival Meeting, whilst the Arkle Novices' Chase is run at Leopardstown annually. The horse was the subject of a song by Dominic Behan and of a Republic of Ireland postage stamp issued in 1981 to mark the 25th anniversary of his retirement. After his death, Arkle's skeleton was put on display at the Museum at the Irish National Stud, Tully, Co. Kildare. Sold for £11000

At Cheltenham, commercial manager Peter McNiele was also deeply involved in Arkle memorabilia.

'In the late 1980s we decided to revamp and redecorate the Arkle bar as part of the third stage of the racecourse redevelopment. We knocked out the old pillars in the Arkle bar and put in memorabilia. We placed a note in the *Racing Post* and that brought in some interesting stuff.

'One great treat, when I was tasked with decorating the bar, was going first to the Dreapers and then to lunch with the Duchess in Cheshire, with Edward [Gillespie, Cheltenham managing director, now retired]. It was wholly entertaining; the room was full of beautiful furniture, five Gold Cups, two Grand National trophies and many others.

'I admired a magnificent canvas on the wall above the sideboard and remarked, "It looks like a Stubbs."

"Well, yes, it is," the Duchess replied.

'Among the memorabilia that the Duchess gave was a Braille poem; we placed it in a glass frame and screwed it to the bar door, but someone ripped it off at one of the meetings, I felt really bad about that. She also gave us the x-ray of Arkle's broken pedal bone, a long reel of film and endless correspondence.

'The Duchess was a very graceful lady, charming. She and the Queen Mother together were like two peas in a pod, loving the racing, like a couple of wonderful old ladies.'

Peter McNeile also visited the old British Library when it was on the Edgeware Road to look up newspaper articles about Arkle.

'I would give the relevant dates, and along came a trolley bearing leather-bound copies of the newspapers, and they then photo-copied the ones I needed.'

These are now a principal feature in the Arkle Bar, which was re-opened on the first day of the Festival, 1989.

Lord Vestey, who was chairman of Cheltenham, remembers, 'The bar was terrific; people used to write to me every year to say it was too crowded, but that was part of it.'

Peter McNeile also described some of the businesses spawned by Arkle, some more successful than others.

'Over the years a number of people chanced their arm trying to make money out of him, mostly Irishmen on the make. One time I was asked if we would sell videos of him, the chap then asked if he could store all two thousand copies here; I didn't dig too deep with my questions but I'd say he was dodgy.

'Another time there was a hideous sculpture that someone was trying to sell, it was an embarrassment, like a cartoon character with squashed legs and was a scary thing to look at.

'We had some success with a painting by Peter Biegel of Arkle and Mill House, it was lent by Lady Fermoy, and we got a limited edition done in aid of the Injured Jockeys Fund. Once we had the print I took about 200 to Ireland for Pat Taaffe and Willie Robinson to sign at Naas before the Cheltenham Festival. The two of them were in a back room and they went on signing until their pen arms gave up; there was nothing in it for them and the IJF isn't even in Ireland.

'Another very strange Irishman created Arkle phone cards; people had to dial about 65 digits to get their number, it was hilarious.'

The old Irish currency featured different animals on one side of a coin and the one on a half crown (two shillings and sixpence) was of a rather fine looking horse. A friend of mine from County Galway, Tom Walshe, tells me a couple of guys took a stash of them to Cheltenham, and sold them as being of Arkle for five guineas each. When someone asked them what the two S and six D (2s6d) stood for, quick as a flash up came the answer, 'It's Irish for miles and furlongs.'

GRAHAM BUDD AUCTIONS, LONDON, NOVEMBER 2012 LOT 19 THE ARKLE BRIDLE

The Arkle Bridle, an authenticated bridle fixed with original reins worn by Arkle in some of his races, the bit inscribed ARKLE 19.4.1957, RETIRED 8.10.68; sold together with a frame mounted with all the original authentication relating to the sale of the bridle at a charity auction in 1970, including a signed letter of authenticity from T W (Tom) Dreaper on Greenogue headed paper dated 26th November 1970; a related letter from Anthony Fairbairn Secretary of the Racegoers Club, 42 Portman Square; the original purchase cheque made payable to the Arkle Memorial Fund; a press cutting regarding the Arkle Auction; and other items (2)

The bridle was bought at a charity auction following a gala performance of the play 'The Jockey Club Stakes' at the Vaudeville Theatre, London, 9th November 1970. The evening was organised by the Racegoers Club as a principal money raiser for the appeal to erect a Doris Lindner-sculpted statue of Arkle at Cheltenham Racecourse, which of course came to fruition. The auction was conducted by the BBC commentator Peter Bromley and three items of Arkle memorabilia were auctioned. This bridle fetched £150 (although reported as guineas), a silver salver set with one of Arkle's shoes made £280, whilst Pat Taaffe's riding boots were purchased by the Duchess of Westminster for 100 pounds.

Sold for £8800

LOT 185

A 1963 Hennessy Gold Cup race card featuring Mill House's defeat of Arkle, sold together with 5 non-Festival Cheltenham racecards from the same National Hunt Season including the inaugural running of

the Massey-Ferguson Gold Cup (now the Boylesports.com Gold Cup)
won by the Irish-trained Limeking.

Sold for £110

ADAMS SALE, DUBLIN, APRIL 30, 2013
LOT 575
ESTIMATE EUR : €300.00 - €500.00
AUCTION DATE : 30-04-2013

Description DESMOND SNEE (20th/21st CENTURY) Portrait
heads of 'Dawn Run' and 'Arkle' Oil on board, 23 x 29cm each Signed
and inscribed (2) A set of Mrs Charmian D Hill's racing colours inset -
These two pictures, painted to Tony Sweeney's commission, are dedicated
to the best chasers, male and female, bred in Ireland in the 20th cen-
tury. In each instance their careers ended prematurely, Arkle's through
injury incurred in the King George VI Chase at the 1966 Christmas
meeting at Kempton Park; and that of Dawn Run through death on a
summer's day in France. Provenance: The estate of Tony Sweeney.

Hammer Price: €800.00

Fan David Adamson from Northern Ireland remembers meeting another remarkable Arkle memorabiliast, W.J. Watson.

'My wife Rosaleen and her mother spotted in a church magazine that this man had not only sculpted Arkle out of solid wood, but in doing so had visited the horse to ensure his scale of the horse was perfect.

'This man welcomed me into his home telling stories of the great horse and forever showing me pieces of memorabilia in the form of trays, cups, ties, tea towels and various other items produced in honour of the horse.

'My visits to a beautiful townland close to Ballymoney in Northern Ireland became a monthly journey of the utmost pleasure. W.J. showed and bred hackney ponies and his knowledge of all things horses was just immense. He spoke of the presence Arkle had in the yard where he was stabled and somehow conveyed the spirit that centred on racing in Ireland in the sixties as one horse alone dominated all the headlines.

'After more than a year of my visits W.J. gave me the first of many gifts which I treasure to this day, a piece of Arkle's tail, a pictorial magazine dedicated to Arkle published in the sixties and a hand painted tie which W.J. painted himself, not to mention a watercolour painting of the great one's head proudly hanging in my house today.

'He would never sell any of his works, but he occasionally gave items to auction for charity and a number to friends as well.'

There is barely a pub or country home in Ireland without at least one picture of Arkle gracing its walls, and many in England, too. Even so, something can still come as a surprise, as it did for Tom Dreaper's daughter, Eva Kauntze about ten years ago.

'I was sitting at the bar in a pub called Simons in Wexford town when suddenly I saw a lifesize photo of Dad looking out at me from the wall – that was eerie.'

CHAPTER 16

ARKLE IN ASHBOURNE

It was in about 2009 that P.J. Durkan, a prime mover behind the GAA in Ashbourne, approached Paddy Woods and suggested the town should really have a statue of its most famous son, Arkle.

There are a number of statues around of famous racehorses – Arkle has one at Cheltenham, of course, along with Dawn Run, Best Mate and Golden Miller; Desert Orchid at Kempton and Red Rum at Aintree. The idea behind the new statue of Arkle is to have it in a public place where it can be seen and admired on a daily basis, and is local to where he was born, reared and trained, unlike a racecourse statue where it is only seen a few times a year.

Paddy Woods agreed it was a great idea and discussed it with the Dreaper family who also liked the plan; a committee was formed with Jim Dreaper as chairman. The chief factor would be how to fund the project, and with this in mind they brought in a key player to help, Greenogue neighbour retired Garda Commissioner Pat Byrne. As Paddy Woods says, 'We wanted a fellow with a bit of clout.'

Pat Byrne retired in 2003 after seven years in the top job. From west

Cork originally, he has lived in the Ashbourne area since 1995. In 2004 he joined the board of Fairyhouse and became chairman in 2010.

'I had no horse involvement other than the love of them, and of racing. Fairyhouse was keen to give a strong signal that it was governed by local people because it had gained an elitist image.'

Pat Byrne not only had a fondness for horses, he had established the Garda mounted unit during his tenure. He was also an Arkle fan.

'There weren't many TVs in west Cork so I used to listen to his races on the radio, and then watched him on Pathé News in Dunmanway cinema. Arkle grabbed everybody's attention, and there was not much else going on anywhere in the country. I remember the Irish Grand National as a big talking point and also especially Cheltenham. He was an icon in terms of the challenge between the two countries, there was big rivalry.'

Having agreed to set up a fund to raise the money for an Arkle statue in Ashbourne, various decisions had to be made: who should sculpt it, how would the money be raised, where would the statue be sited.

Pat Byrne drew up a list of people who might contribute, and also organised house to house collections.

'So many people came on board, in spite of the times,' he says.

Jim Dreaper approached the Duchess of Westminster Foundation, (the Duchess had died in Lochmore in August 2003, aged eighty-eight.) The Foundation sent somebody over to check the bona fides of the scheme, to see the proposed location and to assess the commitment of the local authority, and the accounting process. Once they were satisfied that everything was in order, about twelve months later, the Foundation gave a substantial donation.

Paddy Woods approached Dermot Weld who gave him the name of sculptor Emma MacDermott; she had produced a quarter-size bronze of Blue Wind for Dermot. Her life-size bronzes include Sadler's Wells for Coolmore Stud, Vintage Crop and Michael Kinane for Michael Smurfit and Nijinsky for Vincent O'Brien, along with a number for Sheikh Mohammed al Maktoum, and others worldwide.

One of the first decisions, and quite possibly the best, was that the Arkle statue should be of horse AND rider; the unmistakeable profile of Pat Taaffe riding Arkle brings the bronze truly to life. The end result is a huge tribute to the pair and a real feather in sculptor Emma Mac-Dermott's hat.

Emma hails from Wexford and Dorset, and was already an Arkle fan. She remembers seeing him when she was a member of the Kildare Hunt branch of the Pony Club.

'I was out hunting with my parents one day when I was very small, and we went through Bryanstown. Arkle was there, peering out over the stable door, and there were lots of oohs and aahs and gaping.

'In the Pony Club our Kildare District Commissioner was Brigit O'Brien-Butler. She lived next door to the Taaffes and she often told us how good they were. I also remember Arkle parading in the Dublin Horse Show. Arkle was second only to the Pope in Ireland – nowadays he would probably be well ahead of the Pope!'

Sculpting is an expensive business and money, as ever, reared its ugly head, but Emma, thrilled to be asked to do Arkle, agreed to do it for a rock-bottom price. She told the fund organisers that she would need a year.

One of the problems facing Emma was that her subject was no longer alive; she had seen the skeleton, she had photographs, and she had measurements – vital statistics – that were recorded and reproduced in Ivor Herbert's 1966 book about Arkle, which gave minute detail such as 'width between eyes 8 inches,' 'girth 79 inches' [sometimes given as 80 inches, but in any case, very large]; circumference of jaw 37 ½ inches; hip to ground 63 inches, and so on. For some reason, probably because of his fame and to record them for posterity, the measurements were taken by vet Maxie Cosgrove five days before Arkle won the 1965 King

George VI Chase.

Firstly Emma MacDermott made a quarter lifesize model and from there progressed to the life-size.

She describes how she saw Arkle, 'The exceptional thing is that he's very correct, except that he had an upside down neck and high head carriage – Pat Taaffe's knees were forwards of his shoulder.

'I can just remember Pat Taaffe, and his gentle, shy smile and lovely face. He was a hero.'

Emma described how she has made her statue of Arkle: first there was a welded steel armature, with a double support in the middle and a certain amount of wire. Onto this she put a ton of clay, physically hard work and in which it was essential that she placed it firmly enough to stick tightly. Only then did she begin to fashion Arkle's features, by hand, onto the damp clay, moulding it into the incredibly lifelike figures of both the horse and rider.

Emma acknowledges that the whole statue project owes much to the hard work and enthusiasm of Lynsey Dreaper, including the special fund raising day at Bellewstown races at which Emma was one of the guests in August 2011, along with Lester Piggott. The highlight was the 'Foleys Antiques Support the Arkle Memorial Statue Fund Maiden' featuring ten celebrity jockeys of former years. Much of the day revolved around remembering Arkle, with a large marquee, information about the statue, and a beautifully-produced commemorative race card.

There were ten runners for the Arkle statue race, the most senior of the riders was Arthur Moore, a top Irish trainer and former winning rider of the Irish Grand National on King's Sprite in 1971, and twice trainer of the winner, with Feathered Gale in 1996, and Organisedconfusion in 2011 who was ridden by his niece, Nina Carberry; he has also twice trained the winner of the Irish Arkle Chase.

The winner of the night's one mile six furlong race was Conor O'Dwyer who in his race-riding days had won both the Cheltenham Gold Cup and Champion Hurdle twice each: Imperial Call 1996, War of Attrition 2006, and Hardy Eustace 2004 and 2005. Second was Norman Williamson who had in the past achieved the rare distinction of winning the Gold Cup and Champion Hurdle in the same year, 1995, with Master Oats and Alderbrook.

Adrian Maguire turned back the clock to finish third; another who is now also a trainer, he won the 1991 Irish Grand National as an amateur on Omerta and as a professional the Cheltenham Gold Cup with Cool Ground (1992) and the Queen Mother Champion Chase (Viking Flagship, 1994).

Joe Byrne was riding in the 1970s and 80s mainly for Noel Meade; he won both the Galway Plate and Galway Hurdle in 1984, and he finished fourth in this special race. Fifth home came Jason Titley who had won the Aintree Grand National on Royal Athlete in 1995 and the Irish Grand National two years later with Mudahim, both for trainer Jenny Pitman.

The remaining riders, all of whom raised money for the fund (Gerry Dowd did particularly well), were Robbie Hennessy, originally apprenticed to Tom Dreaper's son-in-law Michael Kauntze; nine times Irish champion jockey Charlie Swan who won the Champion Hurdle three times on Istabraq and the Irish Grand National on Ebony Jane (1993); and Dermot McLoughlin, whose father Liam was the first man to win on Arkle. Dermot himself rode a number of winners for Jim Dreaper.

The cast was completed by Gerry Dowd who also worked for Jim Dreaper for most of his racing life, and rode Brown Lad to the third of his three Irish Grand National victories in 1978.

The whole evening was excellent publicity for the Arkle memorial statue fund and donations rolled in. Robert Hall and Ted Walsh played their part by publicising it on RTÉ television as well. By the start of 2013 sufficient funds had been raised and the actual statue of Arkle was in a Dublin foundry, virtually completed and only awaiting finishing touches. Bureaucracy was a slower matter.

Extensive liaison was undertaken with Meath County Council, with the Dreapers' daughter Lynsey playing a pivotal role, and eventually planning permission was granted outside Supervalu at the Slane end of the main street. The council agreed to be responsible for the site and associated expenses – its security, preparation, design and development – and to include a rail around it and security cameras. The Arkle committee would be responsible for the statue itself.

The site includes an old low wall that was part of the original Ward Union Hunt kennels, and Lynsey is retaining this for its historic interest. She has also been visiting local schools to tell the pupils about Arkle, and why his statue will be in their town.

Difficulties occurred along the way. For one thing, the council found itself short of the money needed to fulfil their side of the obligation. The plot itself was bought from the shopping centre by the county council, but they found themselves unable to do the groundwork and landscaping and this has resulted in a delay. Legal matters also began to cause delay; the lease was to be for ninety-nine years but the council wanted to know what would happen when that expired. As none of the current players would be around, the committee's reaction was 'so what?'

Paddy Woods said, 'We are providing the greatest attraction for Ashbourne. The statue will stand out, broadside to the traffic so it will be seen coming up the street from either direction. It will enhance the overall development of the main street.'

The committee also hopes to start a small museum in the town library and may in time have Arkle's skeleton, if it's moved from the Irish National Stud.

One of the most amusing publicity enterprises came in the 2012 St Patrick's Day parade in Ashbourne when Paddy Woods led the parade on 'Arkle'.

He had to try and find a suitable lookalike, but the first horse he was offered was coloured (that is, skewbald or piebald); no thoroughbreds are of mixed colour (originally associated with gypsy horses), which Arkle certainly wasn't.

Eventually a horse of the right colour was found, but it was a mare! Paddy, who hadn't ridden for years, borrowed her anyway (from Johnny O'Connell of the Kilronan Riding Centre), and just hoped nobody would notice the sex.

The mare was plaited up, and Paddy borrowed a set of Arkle's colours from Jim Dreaper, while jockeys' valet Dave Fox supplied him with breeches, boots and skull cap etc.

As I write, it is still hoped to have the unveiling during 2013; having seen the likeness to both Arkle and Pat Taaffe the statue is certain to be met with universal acclaim. It really is as if the old team have been re-united.

One day Willie Mullins was in the foundry on other business and saw the statue. Ireland's all-conquering trainer says, 'The way it has been done, complete with Pat Taaffe is unbelievable, it beats all.'

CHAPTER 17

THE ARKLE CHASES – LEOPARDSTOWN AND CHELTENHAM

There are two prestigious chases named in honour of Arkle, at Cheltenham in March and at Leopardstown in January and over the years they have both produced winners worthy of following in the footsteps of 'Himself,' not least the two most recent ones.

The owners of the 2013 Leopardstown Arkle Chase, Niall Reilly and Aidan Shiels were lifelong Arkle devotees: the first thing they do when they make their annual pilgrimage to Cheltenham is go and touch Arkle's statue.

On 26 January 2013, the two friends flew in from New York to Dublin and spent the morning at Greenogue. There they looked at a young horse and admired Box number 7, Arkle's old stable. They had hoped to watch a runner of theirs in the point-to-point at Tyrella, Northern Ireland, but the meeting was cancelled – which was just as well, really, as the main reason for their visit was to see their older horse, Benefficient, contest the Arkle Chase at Leopardstown – and that had been brought forward from Sunday to this day, again because of the weather.

Even so, it was a miracle that racing went ahead. The meeting survived an 8am inspection, two chase fences were omitted on the track – and just three horses stood their ground for the two-mile one furlong novice contest in memory of Arkle. Sponsored by Frank Ward Solicitors, the Leopardstown Arkle Chase included a cup presented by the late Anne, Duchess of Westminster.

For Frank Ward, sponsoring the Arkle Novice Chase at Leopardstown was an easy choice. He grew up in Arkle country, hunted with the Ward Union Staghounds who criss-cross the Meath countryside at high speed and with considerable derring-do, and Arkle was an integral part of his young life, remained a passion, and, he felt, represented the best.

The odds-on favourite in 2013 was Arvika Ligeonniere for trainer Willie Mullins, but after jumping the first five fences perfectly he 'put in a short one' and paid the penalty at the next, crumpling on landing and pitching himself and jockey Paul Townend into the sodden ground unscathed. This left Jessie Harrington's Oscars Well splashing through the puddles but as they approached the last fence Benefficient, patiently ridden by Bryan Cooper had joined them. Oscars Well, a former Grade 1 hurdle winner like the Tony Martin-trained Benefficient, made a hash of the last and all but came down; jockey Robbie Power defied gravity to stay in the saddle, but his chance was gone and Benefficient sauntered to his first Grade 1 chase win. At seven, he was a year younger than his two rivals and he was the 10-1 outsider of the three.

Winning the 'Arkle' was an appropriate reward for the joint owners, New Yorkers, Niall Reilly and Aidan Shiels.

Both men hail originally from close to Arkle territory, but they emigrated to New York a number of years back, Niall from Julianstown in Meath, and Aidan from Delvin in the north of Westmeath.

Aidan's venture into racehorse ownership began when he bought a horse at Tattersalls Sales at Fairyhouse, County Meath, put it with Tony Martin to train, and then Aidan, a New York publican, roped in concrete businessman Niall Reilly; and their Northern Alliance won the 2009 Kerry National in Listowel.

The next stop for Benefficient was the Cheltenham NH Festival in March 2013 when, naturally, Niall and Aidan, accompanied by their wives, crossed the pond once more. They opted for the Jewson (Golden Miller) Novice Chase and, at 20-1 Benefficient confirmed that his Leopardstown Arkle win had been no fluke. He led the thirteen-runner field under young Bryan Cooper for most of the race, was overtaken three out but challenged again at the last, regained the lead and ran on stoutly up the hill to beat the hot favourite, Dynaste. His three Grade 1 wins have come at 50-1 (Deloitte Novice Hurdle at Leopardstown), 10-1 and 20-1 – but presumably punters may now wake up to the fact that the beautifully-bred Benefficient (by Beneficial out of a Supreme Leader mare) is a good horse in his own right.

In taking this longer race, they had bypassed the Cheltenham Arkle Chase, and its odds-on favourite, the stunning grey, Simonsig, on the opening day, Tuesday 12 March 2013.

Early racegoers were greeted by the sight of the normal green sward of Cheltenham's two racetracks covered in black, every square inch of the famous turf hidden under frost covers (about forty-five acres in all), making the hallowed course look more like a tarmacadammed Grand Prix circuit than the world's headquarters of National Hunt racing.

At 5.30am the ground temperature was minus 12 degrees centigrade under those covers. A further inspection was called for 8am. Two patches of ground were still frozen and another inspection was called for 10.30am. After that one, racing was on, but put back half an hour and the time of the cross-country chase (which had its own challenging course in the middle of the track) rescheduled to be the last race if the ground survivesda further inspection at 1.40. It didn't, and the chase was further rescheduled for two days later, on Thursday.

By the skin of its teeth, the opening day went ahead; without those vast covers, racing would not have been possible. The traditional roar of the 56,284 crowd echoed round the mighty bowl that is Prestbury Park below Cleeve Hill as the first race got under way.

The Arkle Chase followed and all eyes were on Simonsig, winner of eight of his nine races under Rules; he was second in the other. A beautiful grey with attractive darker dappling, unfashionably bred on heavy East Sussex clay and by a first season sire Fair Mix, Simonsig's connections originally hoped he might win a lowly point-to-point (he did; he won two of three and fell in the other.) Not surprisingly, he was odds-on to win the seven-runner Arkle Chase; but he didn't have it all his own way. For the first time he found a contest on his hands. He fought for his head, pulling strongly against jockey Barry Geraghty's valiant attempts to restrain him, to conserve his energy for the moment that matters, the finish. He was finding himself under pressure and on the far side made a serious mistake, forcing Barry Geraghty to employ all the techniques of his trade to keep the partnership intact. He swooped into the lead three out, made another error at the second last, but his class and experience tell, and he galloped up the hill to become the latest on The Arkle's roll of honour, to the delight of trainer Nicky Henderson, whose fifth 'Arkle' this was, and owner Ronnie Bartlett.

Simonsig was bred by Simon Tindall, from Mayfield in East Sussex and his early education was undertaken by Nick Pearce, a point-to-point rider from nearby Crowborough. He has produced some fifty-plus point-to-point winners for Simon Tindall, but writes on his website, 'Simonsig is the best by far, his natural ability and class from day one were obvious. From the day I broke him in he was electric, it was hard work restraining myself not to let the handbrake off too soon when we started working him at four.

Hailing from Airdrie, Lanarkshire, owner Ronnie Bartlett is an international potato king supplying retailers from Jersey, Europe and the U.S., as well as growing his own potatoes on a thousand acres in East Anglia.

He already owned a half-brother to Simonsig, Clausen, who won a point-to-point and placed three times, and so his agent Michael Stroud spoke to breeder Simon Tindall about buying Simonsig and, once purchased, he sent him to Ian Ferguson in Northern Ireland to point-to-point.

After Simonsig had won the Racing Post Point-to-Point Champion Bumper at Fairyhouse, his new owner thought he could be something special and he sent him to trainer Nicky Henderson. Not surprisingly, he now says, 'He's my best horse ever, there aren't many like him.'

 filename

Soon after this race two of horse-racing's all time greats sat together in the Arkle Bookshop, a small marquee beside the Arkle statue overlooking the paddock. Nonagenarian Sir Peter O'Sullevan, universally acknowledged as the greatest commentator of all time and whose husky, supremely professional tones have been revered for over half a century, sits beside legendary flat race jockey, Lester Piggott, winner of nine Derbies. Their heads are down, signing their respective books, but every few minutes they pause and catch each other's eye as old friends do. They smile, and the crowd jostles some more, waving their digital cameras aloft and snapping away.

Sir Peter's smile is open and wide and benevolent and there is a twinkle in his eye; he is a truly special man with a life well lived. If Lester was not renowned for smiling you would not know that here, for he is in fact grinning. Two elderly men who reached the pinnacles of their respective careers, now relaxed and looking mildly surprised at the attention; they are a credit to the whole sport of horseracing and the wider world – just as Arkle was.

Twelve days later Sir Peter, ninety-five, suffered a mild stroke and although he returned home after less than a week in hospital it caused him to miss the Grand National meeting at Aintree.

Another landmark was achieved on Arkle day at Cheltenham. Tom Dreaper's Irish record for training the most Festival winners, twenty-six, was finally broken. The new holder is the all conquering Willie Mullins who trains over a hundred horses in County Carlow, with twenty-nine. Tom Dreaper never had more than thirty-five horses in training. Of his twenty-six Festival wins, four of them were from Arkle. For many years Fulke Walwyn held the overall record with forty. In 2012, Nicky Henderson's seven winners took him to forty-six, and four more in 2013 brought up the half century by, appropriately, Bobs Worth in the Cheltenham Gold Cup.

The Arkle Chase at Cheltenham has produced some great winners over the years, but is mostly known as a pointer to future Queen Mother Champion Chase winners. It seems strange that the two-mile former Cotswold Chase was chosen to bear Arkle's name, given he was best remembered over three miles. That does not detract from past winners, notably Remittance Man, Klairon Davis, Flagship Uberalles, Moscow Flyer (twice), Azertyuiop, Voy Por Ustedes, Sizing Europe and, most recently, Sprinter Sacre who all went on to win 'the Queen Mother'. Alverton is the only Arkle winner to have gone on to take the Gold Cup, although the 2005 Gold Cup winner Kicking King had finished second in the Arkle the previous year (to Well Chief).

Captain Chris won in 2011 and ran unplaced in the 2013 Gold Cup, while the 2012 running belonged to possibly the most exciting horse of all to emerge since Arkle, Sprinter Sacre.

I have to add an amusing tale of the 1994 Arkle Chase winner, Nakir, owned by Jim Lewis who is best remembered for his triple Gold Cup winner Best Mate. French-bred by the Aga Khan, Nakir went straight into novice chases in 1994, winning all four, the third of which was The Arkle, in the hands of Jamie Osborne.

It was Jim Lewis' first Festival winner and as such his most exciting racing experience to that date.

The Duchess of Westminster presented the bronze trophy of Arkle, and connections posed for photographs with her. As they were doing so, the Duchess whispered into Jim's ear, 'Mr Lewis, I think I had better hold on to this trophy, I can feel you trembling from here.' It was very heavy!

CHAPTER 18

REMEMBERING ARKLE

Throughout this celebration of Arkle's life, timed to commemorate the fiftieth anniversary of his first Cheltenham Gold of March 1964, we have seen many heartfelt tributes to the great horse, but I can't resist closing with a few more from those who saw him; the great and the good in racing plus 'Joe Public' fans – and even so, this is only a selection (in alphabetical order):

David Adamson, a fan: I was only nine years of age when Arkle won his first Gold Cup so my memory is pretty vague on how I came to worship the horse that was to become simply known as Himself. My late Father often spoke of him as more of a friend than just a horse to wager a few pounds on and that really cemented my informative days of Arkle's triumphs in glorious black & white. I was fascinated and wanted to know just what made this horse tick and gathered up endless articles about his extraordinary racing feats, his trainer, work rider, the owner and the breeding lines.

Lord Patrick Beresford, former amateur who rode against Arkle: He would have won the Aintree Grand National standing on his head.

James Burns, trainer, born the year of Arkle's third Gold Cup: Arkle was a mythical horse.

TP Burns, retired champion flat jockey who rode Arkle to win his only flat race: Arkle was an exceptional horse.

Pat Byrne, retired Garda Commissioner: Arkle was an icon.

The late **Tom Dreaper**, speaking on film prior to a possible comeback: You don't have to teach a fifth year university student how to spell.

Valerie Percy (née Dreaper), trainer's younger daughter: I never saw him run because I was away at school, it was just one of those things, but I did ride him bareback up the road, led off a headcollar, when he was being roughed off and going out to grass.

I was working for Dot Love [trainer of 2013 Irish Grand National winner Liberty Counsel] as a nanny/au pair/mucker outer when my father died [in 1975].

Hellen Egan, Parts Inventory Analyst, Australia, who as a student helped assemble Arkle's skeleton: I will definitely enjoy the story of the horse I helped put together in the museum.

Mick Foster, musician, half of the world famous Foster and Allen: I was a teenager but we were all fans of Arkle, he was the greatest thing since sliced bread, and being from Kildare, I was a huge Pat Taaffe fan.

Eddie Harty, retired jockey: Arkle was the finest steeplechaser and Pat Taaffe a fine horseman, they had a unique partnership. Arkle was built like an athlete; he was a peacock, a racing machine and it is a privilege to have seen him.

Nicky Henderson, trainer: Arkle was the absolute legend and to me he still is; there won't be another. It's about time we were reading about him again.

Michael Hourigan, trainer: I was young and ambitious and wanted to be a flat jockey. Of course Arkle inspired me. As I got older I rode in some races with Pat Taaffe, a real gentleman. I was riding in Killarney and dropped my whip three out, Pat was just ahead of me but beaten and dropping back; I shouted at him to lend me his whip. He passed it, our fingers touched, but the whip slipped to the ground – I finished second.

Timmy Hyde, retired jockey, owner of Camas Park Stud: There was never a horse like him and there never will be again because of the lumps of weight he gave away.

Michael Kauntze, retired Flat trainer, son-in-law of Tom Dreaper: I remember quite clearly being absolutely certain that Arkle went down the back straight at Sandown (over seven fences) faster than the three-year-old Classic aspirants did in the following Derby trial!

Peadar Kelly, Kelly's Pub, Ashbourne: We still get journalists here from England looking for Arkle information.

Ted Kelly, retired Turf Club vet and stipendary steward: You have to put it down to the genius of the man that he took Arkle straight to Cheltenham [for his first chase] – but then he was so well schooled at home.

Tommy Kinane, retired professional jockey who rode against Arkle: Arkle had a huge heart; stand out were his three Gold Cups and Pat Taaffe sending him off at the last.

Tom Lacy, retired trainer who rode against Arkle: Arkle was the real deal.

Jim Lewis, owner of triple Gold Cup winner Best Mate: During the mighty Arkle's pomp I was still playing football on Saturdays but I was there at Cheltenham when he won his third Gold Cup and also witnessed his finest hour at Sandown Park [Gallaher], it was total confirmation of his superiority. When you look at what he achieved he was on his own; Best Mate was just a good horse that everyone loved.

'The mighty Arkle was a colossus, out on his own; inevitably after Best Mate won his third Gold Cup people were bound to draw comparisons, but that is ludicrous. Best Mate deserves to be in the Parthenon with Arkle, but he was never asked to carry all that weight.

Johnny Lumley, Arkle's lad: Mill House was much bigger, but when

Arkle walked in [to the paddock] he didn't look it. Arkle floated like a ballerina with his head held high and he looked as big. He knew he was important and the best.

Steven Mair, UK fan: my memories of Arkle are tinged with a little regret in that I failed to appreciate him as much as I should have when he was active. The reason was that I loved Mill House and I was devastated when he lost that 64 Gold Cup to the Irish horse; I was 10 years old.

I still retained hopes the following year when rushing home from school for the 65 renewal but Mill House was crushed; he had been well beaten by Arkle in the Hennessy in between. So, I have always felt I short-changed myself when Arkle was in his pomp.

Peter McNeile, Director of Sponsorship, Cheltenham: At no time since Arkle have I ever come across the same magnetism or seen so much commerciality spawned as there was for Arkle – and they all had a story.

Noel Meade, trainer: His first Gold Cup really caught the public's imagination; when he made that mistake in his third one, Pat Taaffe was ready for him, even though he'd never made an error like that before.

Stan Mellor, retired champion jockey and jockey coach: Arkle was an amazing horse; he wasn't finished by any means when he broke his pedal bone.

Maureen Mullins, widow of champion trainer Paddy and mother and grandmother of trainers and jockeys: There will never be another Arkle, he was so much ahead of even our best – look at what he pulled out against our Height O' Fashion [the mare was trained firstly by the Mullins and then the Lacys] and we won thirteen races with her [including the Irish Cesarewitch on the Flat] – and Arkle was far ahead of Kauto Star and Best Mate. And the way Arkle walked – he out-stepped the Duchess.

Willie Mullins, champion Irish trainer: Another Arkle? Never, but every owner says their horse will be the next Arkle! There will never be another like him again for a proper staying chaser, it would be hard to see one as good as him either side of the Irish Sea.

Noel O'Brien, Senior Irish Handicapper: Arkle was awe-inspiring. He was a horse so far ahead, a freak that weights couldn't bring him together with other horses.

Sir Peter O'Sullevan, retired commentator/racing journalist: Of course, 'Himself' meant a great deal to me. What a privilege for a compulsive horse fancier to have lived and worked in an era of an equine for whom the rules of racing had to be re-written to accommodate his talent.

Lester Piggott, legendary retired multiple champion Flat race jockey: He was something else, wasn't he?

Richard Pitman, We have still not seen his equal and until the top chasers attempt to give stones away in handicaps as he did, it is impossible to equate the different eras.

Leo Powell, managing editor, *Irish Field*: While many brilliant chasers have graced the turf before and after Arkle, it is hard to argue against the view that he was simply the best ever. I don't expect to see his like again.

Kevin Prendergast, octogenarian trainer, former amateur jockey who rode against Arkle: We have not seen a better horse in my life.

Will Reilly, freelance broadcaster and betting shop consultant: I found it amusing that Arkle's picture was above them in the background while a stern-faced Simon Crisford, Paul Bittar and two others faced the press on Thursday (*Racing Post*, April 2013) over the Mahmood Al Zarooni anabolic steroids case. Timeless quality underpinned by the manners and horsemanship of a bygone age.

Jim Sheridan, Oscar winning film director: I remember Arkle in black and white. On the little TV my Dad had and with an aerial on the roof. I remember that we did not lose the signal. I remember the sense of pride the Irish had about him. I remember that everybody has more or less forgotten about Mill House who was a great horse. When Arkle ruled he was beyond Muhammad Ali, beyond any sportsman or animal wonder. He had majesty. For the Irish who under the Penal Laws could only own a horse worth five pounds his victory was like water to a man in the Sahara. I believe that horses are the first real Irish business. Banned under the Penal Laws but necessary to the English in the Napoleonic Wars. So out of that we were allowed our horses. And before the horse power of steam, horse power was everything. Arkle was horse power in flight. He was our Centaur. He hurt nobody and he took no prisoners. God will be good to him.

Patsy Smiles, retired trainer's secretary: My best memories of him were not racing, but going out with the string to the gallops where he had to walk on quite away ahead of the string as he was so keen, and that very high, eager head carriage he had – he seemed to know that he was simply the best!

The late **Pat Taaffe**, speaking on film: He can accelerate out of trouble; he's an easy horse to ride; it's like putting your foot down on a Rolls Royce.

Tom Taaffe, Cheltenham Gold Cup winning trainer and son of Arkle's principal jockey Pat: Arkle was part and parcel of growing up; my parents would go to Cheltenham every March and come back with two, three or four winners, it was just normal.

We are never going to see an Arkle again because we won't have a horse that takes on the challenges that he did.

David Tatlow, five times British champion point-to-point rider during Arkle's heyday, top show rider and producer and all-round horseman: Arkle was unbelievable, it was a magic era.

Ted Walsh, trainer, TV racing presenter, former champion amateur rider: I was a teenager and I remember all his races, but for a short time Flyingbolt was better than Arkle.

The late **Duchess of Westminster**, speaking on film: My best memory is his first Gold Cup, I shall never forget the noise – I think I was making quite a lot of it.

Ronnie White, clockmaker, Mullingar: Everyone knew of Arkle, like the Titanic, you don't have to be horsey to know of him.

CHAPTER 19

WOULD-BE ARKLES

'People are always comparing different generations, but that is almost impossible and can be odious.'

Many racing followers concur with this view of Irish Senior Handicapper Noel O'Brien, who adds, 'I look at Arkle's weight-carrying performances: for any horse to be able to give that amount and be beating horses of high standard puts him without doubt on the highest pedestal. Arkle gave 35lbs to Stalbridge Colonist when beaten by half a length, yet Stalbridge Colonist went on to finish second and third in the next two Gold Cups. I look at that and gasp.'

The rankings system reflects the highest ever rating given to a horse at any time in his career.

FLYINGBOLT (1960s)

In 1948 a private handicapper and professional punter by the name of Phil Bull began publishing annual ratings which morphed into the eponymous Timeform series. A mathematics graduate, Phil Bull wanted to establish a mathematical link to a horse's performance, based on the time the horse recorded.

Only two years younger than Arkle, Flyingbolt remains the highest rated horse by Timeform after Arkle, with Arkle on 212 and Flyingbolt on 210. Of the rest in the next dozen only third-rated Sprinter Sacre (see below) and Long Run (see below) are still racing. Sprinter Sacre may yet go up from his 192, which is one ahead of both Kauto Star (see below) and Mill House, who shares a chapter.

Flyingbolt has come into the Arkle story several times. Stable companions in adjacent boxes, they were both looked after by Johnny Lumley.

Paddy Woods was riding Arkle with Pat Taaffe on Flyingbolt when they had their hair-raising, never-to-be-repeated schooling session. Flyingbolt won first time out, in a bumper ridden by Alan Lillingston and he remained unbeaten in Ireland for nearly two years. The English bred, Irish produced Flyingbolt (by Derby winner Airborne) won the same Broadway Novices Chase at Cheltenham as Arkle, and like him also numbered on his CV the Leopardstown Chase, Thyestes Chase and Irish Grand National (in which Height O'Fashion finished second receiving a whopping 40lbs, just 2lbs less than three stone). In 1965 he won the Cotswold Chase and Massey Ferguson Chase (carrying 12 stone 6lbs and sploshing through water lying on the track) and the Black and White Whiskey Gold Cup at Ascot, but it is Flyingbolt's performance during the 1966 Cheltenham Festival that stands out. He not only won the Two-Mile [Queen Mother] Champion Chase by a stunning fifteen lengths, but the very next day turned out again for the Champion Hurdle, no less. He led over the last flight, to be outpaced on the run to the line by Salmon Spray and Sempervivum. The next month he humped a whopping 12 stone 7lbs to win the Irish Grand National to beat the useful Height O'Fashion carrying only 9 stone 9lbs; this was 'Arkle déjà vu' – the other four runners carried 9 stone 7lbs; one of these was Splash (third) who had won the previous year carrying 10 stone 13lbs.

Unfortunately, Flyingbolt contracted the debilitating disease brucellosis, which is more usually associated with cattle, although it can affect humans too. He did not return to form after it, and Tom Dreaper felt he should be retired. The owner, however, sent him to Scotland where his career became intermittent and slid downhill, a sad and ignominious end to a great horse, but he remains the second highest rated chaser to Arkle.

L'ESCARGOT (1970s)

Too often an unsung hero, L'Escargot not only won the Cheltenham Gold Cup twice, but also the Grand National at his fourth attempt. From the start the chestnut gelding by Escart III showed talent, winning his bumper first time out, and then on only his second outing over hurdles he took a division of the Gloucestershire Hurdle (now the Supreme Novices and invariably run as one race), the traditional curtain raiser of the Cheltenham NH Festival.

He won his first Gold Cup in 1970 at odds of 33-1, in spite of having won a chase in America at the end of his novice chasing season, and the W.D. & H.O. Wills Chase final at Haydock. The Gold Cup was a close finish, in which Tommy Carberry and L'Escargot got the better of Pat Taaffe and French Tan.

L'Escargot's 1971 Gold Cup victory came over the Tom Dreaper trained Leap Frog; watching the replay, (and with the benefit of hindsight) L'Escargot looks a little out of love with the game, propping at the last two fences, but he drew clear impressively on the flat. Nevertheless it was his last win for four years.

Trained by Dan Moore at Fairyhouse, L'Escargot was owned by the American Ambassador to Ireland, Raymond Guest, who had already doubly achieved his ambition to win the Derby, with Larkspur and Sir Ivor. In an effort to add the Grand National he bought Flying Wild (who we have come across several times in the Arkle story) but she fell at the first fence. He tried with several more until he was persuaded to let his Gold Cup star attempt the epic race.

L'Escargot had the class and ability but it took Tommy Carberry to cajole him; at his first attempt in 1972 L'Escargot took an instant dislike to Aintree and tried to stop at the third, only to be knocked over there. The following year, Tommy Carberry 'didn't think I would get down to Becher's even in a horsebox.' Yet he 'jumped like a buck' and finished third, giving two stone to the winner, Red Rum who caught the great Crisp on the line. For 1974, he moved up a place, finishing second to Red Rum. By 1975, L'Escargot, now twelve years old, had been without a win for four years and his weight came down accordingly. He thoroughly deserved his victory, ahead of Red Rum. Tommy Carberry said, 'I had to tune in to him. You could feel his class, but he had to be enjoying himself. He was the best horse I ever rode.'

DAWN RUN (1980s)

Twenty years after Arkle won his first Gold Cup in 1964 Dawn Run won the Champion Hurdle (she also won the Champion Hurdles of Ireland and France that year, 1984). It was after her first chase, at Navan in November 1984 that she began to be hailed 'the new Arkle.'

The last chapter of *DAWN RUN The story of a champion racehorse and her remarkable owner* published on the eve of her Cheltenham Gold Cup win was entitled 'In Arkle's Footsteps'. For her first steeplechase in Navan spectators turned out in droves on a wet winter's day, mackintosh collars turned up, and they noticed how Dawn Run looked around her in that same imperious, interested, way that Arkle used to.

She jumped like an old hand and won convincingly in the hands of Tony Mullins over useful rivals Dark Ivy and Buck House. Spectators stampeded to the winners' enclosure and the Press were equally impressed as shown in their headlines: *The Daily Telegraph:* Echoes of Arkle in Dawn Run Victory; *The Irish Times:* Dawn Run has World of Chasing at her Feet; and in their columns, Michael O'Farrell (*Irish Times*), 'it was a privilege to see Dawn Run perform so brilliantly on her first appearance over fences.' When pressed by Buck House, she 'Arkle-like, just went away. Each stag-like jump brought a gasp of admiration from the large crowd who braved the weather to see her run.'

Tony Power, describing Dawn Run's 'spectacular transition' from hurdling to chasing, declared that the winner of the English, Irish and French Champion Hurdles 'must be the most exciting National Hunt horse in training since the balmy days when Arkle bestrode the world of jumping.'

About a month after that race Dawn Run strained a ligament in a pastern and had a year off.

She returned with two Irish chase wins but then unseated in a prep race at Cheltenham, and went to the 1986 Gold Cup after only four steeplechases.

The race produced one of the all time great finishes; she led until the second last, was third and 'beaten' over the last but that assumption did not account for the galvanization of her by Jonjo O'Neill and her incredible guts in responding, to become still the only horse in history to achieve the Champion Hurdle/Gold Cup double. Sadly, three months later when attempting to regain her French crown and jumping with all her panache she 'missed one out' down the back, fell headlong onto her neck and was killed instantly.

Form: 8411104116132121/411211111/1/11UR1F12F

DESERT ORCHID 1980s-90s

In Desert Orchid's early days Dawn Run was his nemesis. They met eight or nine times on the racecourse and she beat him on every occasion (in her 1984 Champion Hurdle he finished eighth). Born in 1979, his career blossomed after hers had literally died and he became one of the most popular steeplechasers ever, helped by being grey, and he made the King George VI Chase at Kempton on Boxing Day his own. From October 1988 to December 1991, he won 13 chases, the first six consecutively; he won the King George in 1986, 1988, 1989 and 1990, and then fell in it in his retirement race in 1991.

He won the Tingle Creek over two miles at Sandown in 1988, proving he had speed as well as stamina, which he demonstrated by winning the 1990 Irish Grand National under top weight.

He won the 1988 Whitbread Gold Cup and he also won the Gold Cup, bravely, in 1989 and was third in the next two years. Although he was wonderfully consistent I don't think notions of comparing him with Arkle were ever taken too seriously, although his rating of 187 puts him in fifth place behind Arkle.

He was a hugely popular horse with the public, and he was a charismatic character and a flamboyant jumper of fences.

His chasing form was: 111111F/1211131/241413/23F/

MOSCOW FLYER LATE 1990s-2000s

Moscow Flyer was almost out of the bargain basement and took a while to mature into a racehorse and a little longer again to get his jumping consistent, but he became one of the best two-mile racehorses of all time. He won the Queen Mother Champion Chase twice and fell in the intervening year.

Moscow Flyer, trained by Jessica Harrington, won twenty-seven of his forty-five races but, like Arkle, he failed to win a bumper. Like him, he matured after a summer at grass following his first season racing. Once he went chasing, he won the first nineteen in which he completed – but he either fell or unseated jockey Barry Geraghty six times, ensuring he always kept his followers on tenterhooks, until such time as he 'grew out' of the habit, as his lifetime form illustrates: 6343/1118/13121F21/F111F11/1U111/U111U1/111111/2245/

There should be a final '1' on this, because in April 2007 he came out of a year long retirement to win the charity flat race at Punchestown for trainer's daughter Kate Harrington, which in itself was a noble feat.

Moscow Flyer might have contested the 2001 Champion Hurdle had it not been cancelled due to the foot and mouth epidemic, and he was bred to stay the extended three miles of the Cheltenham Gold Cup, but it is as a two-mile chaser that he made his name. He won the 2002 'Arkle', and the Queen Mother Champion Chase of 2003, unseated in 2004 and made amends by winning it again in 2005.

His ranking of 184 puts him on the same as Gold Cup winners Burrough Hill Lad and Long Run, seven places behind Arkle.

BEST MATE 2000s

'People often try and compare Arkle with others, but I think that's silly,' says Best Mate's owner, Jim Lewis. 'They were different eras, but when you look at what Arkle achieved he was on his own; Best Mate was just a good horse that everyone loved.'

With three Cheltenham Gold Cups under his belt Best Mate is naturally up there with the Arkle pretenders. He deserves his place nearly at the top of the tree, and he had one of the stronger claims to have been 'the next Arkle'. Apart from his triple success in steeplechasing's blue riband, he was a model of consistency, finishing in first or second place every time he ever ran bar his last, with a ratio of two-thirds wins and one third second. His form, from November 1999 to November 2005 reads: 11221/1112/1221/111/211/12/P/ This included his excursions over hurdles, and the only exception to his 1-2 record was his last race when he collapsed and died; yet, that day he was 'out with the washing' in the betting. He also pulled up in an Irish point-to-point at the start of his career before winning his only other one.

Best Mate was never asked to do what Arkle did: never to run as many times in a season, nor to carry huge weights in handicaps; it was almost as if he was delicate, wrapped in cotton wool – it has been said that running him in Huntingdon and Exeter, his traditional warm up races, were like two gymkhanas to Best Mate – but his consistency at the highest level was outstanding. By his era, top horses had a number of 'conditions' or Pattern races open to them, meaning they seldom had to run in handicaps with huge weights. The Anglo/Irish pattern was set-up in the 1994-1995 season. Best Mate, also, in two books about him was compared with Arkle, and one had a chapter entitled 'The Next Arkle?'

He was one of Arkle's most worthy princes – but it is Arkle who continues to reign as king.

His ranking of 182 puts him in joint twelfth behind Arkle. Like Arkle he never fell on the racecourse.

DENMAN 2000/10s

Denman and Kauto Star, like Arkle and Flyingbolt, were destined to become stable companions and the best around of their era. Unlike Arkle and Flyingbolt they were allowed to race against each other.

Denman won the Cheltenham Gold Cup once, to Kauto's twice, plus Kauto Star's incredible five King George's, (see below), but Denman deserves his place in this line up for being a rare horse of his calibre in the modern era to even try and defy weight in handicaps. He stands out as a horse who, like Arkle, could carry huge weights and still win, though not as often. Noel O'Brien agrees, but adds 'but still at a lower level.'

A big, strong horse – an old-fashioned steeplechaser type – Denman had a massive shoulder which undoubtedly helped him carry big weights. But he was also burdened with ill health, and he was off the course for 11 months between March 2008 and February 2009, having undergone heart surgery following his epic Gold Cup victory over Kauto Star in 2008.

His record in the Cheltenham Gold Cup is excellent: having won it in 2008, he was second to Kauto Star the following year, and to Imperial

Commander in 2010, and he was second again in 2011 to Long Run, with Kauto Star third.

He won many admirers in the Hennessy Gold Cup at Newbury; he ran in it three times, always carrying the now customary top weight of 11 stone 12lbs. He won it as a seven-year-old in 2007, took it again in 2009, and made a valiant attempt in 2010, but faded to third.

Denman, on top weight of 11 stone 12lbs, was the only Gold Cup horse of recent years to have contested and won the Hennessy, until Bobs Worth, 11 stone 6lbs beat Tidal Bay, 11 stone 12lbs in 2012 before taking the Gold Cup in 2013. It is increasingly rare that horses are asked to carry 12 stone – even the level-weighted Cheltenham Gold Cup has been run off 11 stone 10lbs since 2004 , and 12 stone 7lbs is long since gone.

Denman's ranking of 183 puts him joint tenth behind Arkle. His form reads: 1/11112/11111/1111/22F/1U24/325/

KAUTO STAR 2000/10s

There was a notion that precocious French-bred NH horses, which begin their jumping life at the tender age of three, will burn out by the time they are seven or eight. This was well and truly confounded by Kauto Star.

Kauto Star also began his career as a busy three-year-old in France, winning three times at that age. His first English run was a novice chase in Newbury which he won when still only four. He fell in the 2006 Queen Mother Champion Chase, at six years, and won the first of four Betfair's the following November (which he ran in five times but fell in 2008). He took in a Tingle Creek over two miles before winning his first King George (three miles) and rounded off an unbeaten 2006-7 season by beating Exotic Dancer in the Cheltenham Gold Cup.

Although he did not quite match that again, he nevertheless finished first or second in all the top races, except for when he unseated at Haydock and took a horrid fall in the 2010 Gold Cup. When he was twice third to Long Run in the 2011 King George and the Gold Cup, followed by pulling up in Punchestown that May, professional and armchair punters alike were calling for him to be retired.

Trainer Paul Nicholls insisted on waiting to see how he came in from summer grass the following autumn. What followed was one of the most amazing come-backs ever witnessed, a credit to all those around him and in particular to himself.

Kauto Star returned to action in the Betfair Chase at Haydock Park, a traditional route for top class chasers. The young Gold Cup victor Long Run was favourite, but Kauto Star beat him. Perhaps Long Run was a little less fit than the athletic light of former years? But Kauto Star disproved that by beating him again in the King George, winning that race for an incredible fifth time and truly showing aficionados all that is great and good about steeplechasing.

When he pulled up in the following month's Gold Cup time was rightly called on one of the most remarkable of chasing careers. Kauto Star was a smaller, lighter-framed horse than either Long Run or Denman, but he was very athletic and highly talented. He deserved his place as a popular favourite, and is one of the best chasers ever to have graced the turf.

Rated 191, he shares fourth place with Mill House behind Arkle. His form reads: 21/11F2353/112/21F/111111/211122/1U11/11F/133/P11P-

LONG RUN 2010s

After Long Run's Gold Cup win of 2011 at only six years old, his bullish owner Robert Waley-Cohen, now chairman of Cheltenham, predicted he would win it five years in a row. Amateur ridden by the owner's competent son, Sam, Long Run stretched down the final hill at Cheltenham in 2011 and devoured the ground approaching the last two fences behind the two previous winners Kauto Star and Denman. He swept past them imperiously in mid-air at the last fence to gallop to a convincing win, and there were indeed many who wondered if, after four and a half decades, we were truly witnessing 'another Arkle.'

In 2012 he finished third behind Synchronised and he finished in the same position in 2013, behind Bobs Worth. Long Run is a model of consistency, as his form shows: 21211113/1211113/311/2213-2132. French bred, his first twelve races between May 2008 and November 2009 were in Auteuil, six of those as a three-year-old. Between coming to England in December 2009 (when he won a novice chase at Kempton on Boxing Day) to March 2013, he has run a total of thirteen times. At first he made too many jumping errors, but intensive schooling has remedied this, and he has never fallen or unseated.

As I write he still has youth on his side and he could yet notch up another couple of Gold Cups, but he looks more likely to be placed. His King George victory at Kempton on St Stephen's Day/Boxing Day in 2012 was as dour and game as they come, fighting back on the run-in having looked beaten. He had been beaten in the same race by a rejuvenated Kauto Star in 2011 but had also won the 2010 'King George', (which was postponed and was actually run in January 2011.)

A big, good looking horse, Long Run usually contests three or four races per season, and in 2013 he ended with a good second in the 2013 Punchestown Gold Cup (in which Sam Waley-Cohen dropped his whip but showed incredible quick wittedness and gymnastic prowess to catch it *behind* him in mid air on the run in.) Like most of today's top horses, he goes the Pattern route, although he ran in the 2010 Paddy Power Gold Cup at Cheltenham, in which he finished a close third in the 18-runner handicap. He is rated 184 ranking him joint eighth behind Arkle.

SPRINTER SACRE 2010s

Sprinter Sacre is the most exciting horse since Arkle. That observation came before his superb 2013 exploits, and did not emanate from either his trainer Nicky Henderson, or the Champion Chaser's owner, Mrs Caroline Mould, but from Arkle's jockey's son, Tom Taaffe.

'He has a presence like Arkle. Look at him at the finish of a race, not when he comes in, but as he pulls up: he stops and looks around him as only Arkle did. I watched Barry [Geraghty] go to turn him round but Sprinter Sacre just stood there with ears pricked. And this was his first novice chase [at Doncaster]. I just went "wow".

'He is a most exciting horse who cruises and jumps. Nicky Henderson has said he has had nothing to touch Arkle, and Arkle is supreme for what he did: the weights, style, ease, cruising, jumping. Running in handicaps giving so much weight away will never happen again. It's logical for trainers to go the Pattern route – we won't have a future Gold Cup winner running in the Thyestes Chase.

'Arkle was unique for his ability, and fortunate to have a fantastic trainer, rider – and riders – and owner.'

Sprinter Sacre is by a German bred horse, Network, out of a French mare; so far he has been beaten just twice in his life, when second in his first hurdle race, and when beaten into third by Al Ferof in the Supreme Novices Hurdle in Cheltenham, 2011; in his very first race he won by the new official distance of a nose (for which read a whisker, and is shorter than a short head); he had been hampered in running and crucially the close finish appeared not to leave a detrimental mark on him. He beat Cue Card in the 2012 'Arkle' and effortlessly made the graduation to the Queen Mother Champion Chase in 2013.

In this, Sprinter Sacre further stamped his superiority with a stunning victory; his transition to the top class had been so smooth that he scared away a number of possible opponents, just as Arkle used to – and spectators on the packed stands were cheering *before* he had cleared the final fence.

At Aintree (on the Mildmay course) a few weeks later he move up to two and a half miles and met horses like Cue Card within their own comfort zone; Cue Card, much like some of Arkle's opponents, is a top class horse and he had won the two mile five furlong Ryanair Chase at Cheltenham rather than take on Sprinter Sacre. Ireland's Flemenstar, who had by-passed Cheltenham, was also a runner. But, much like Flat star Frankel, when Sprinter Sacre moved up to a longer distance it made no difference. Sprinter Sacre simply sauntered away from his opposition. Connections cannot be accused of wrapping him up in cotton wool, for after Cheltenham and Aintree he travelled over to Punchestown for Ireland's National Hunt Festival, to contest the Irish Champion Chase. His tall, sleek frame looked a picture, and the crowd were lined several deep not only round the paddock but also the saddling enclosure and the walkway out to the course. The ground was heavy and Sizing Europe cut out all the running to the second last. Sprinter Sacre was in the lead by the last and although he didn't so much saunter to victory in the ground it was nevertheless job done – ten wins from ten steeplechases – and a deserved summer holiday coming up. It was a great credit to connections that they brought him over to Ireland.

His form to the end of 2013 reads 11/2113/11111-11111, and is rated 192, with only Flyingbolt and Arkle ahead of him.

CRCR

Arkle remains the highest-rated steeplechaser ever. He was voted the greatest sports personality of the 1960s in Britain ahead of boxer 'I'm the greatest' Mohammad Ali (Cassius Clay) and the footballer who captained England to victory in the 1966 World Cup, Bobby Moore.

In a 2004 *Racing Post* poll, forty years after his first Gold Cup, Arkle topped the list of favourite racehorses ahead of Desert Orchid and Red Rum, both of whom had raced within the memory of many more voters.

Like his contemporaries the Beatles, Arkle – 'Himself' – remains forever Number One to young and old alike.

APPENDIX I:
THE PEDIGREES OF
THE TWO ARKLES

THE 'OTHER' ARKLE

ARKLE (GB) br. H, 1894. 2 starts, unplaced. Career earnings, nil
Breeder, First Duke of Westminster. Owner: Mr. R. and O. Guedes.
Exported to U.S.A. 1899 and then to Argentina in 1908. Stallion at 'Haras Las Porteñas'.

ARKLE

ARKLOW (GB) b. 1889	BEND OR (GB) ch. 1877	DONCASTER (GB) ch. 1870	STOCKWELL (GB) ch. 1849	THE BARON (IRE)	ch. 1842
				POCAHONTAS (GB)	b. 1837
			MARIGOLD (GB) ch. 1860	TEDDINGTON (GB)	ch. 1848
				RATAN MARE (GB)	b. 1852
		ROUGE ROSE (GB) ch. 1865	THORMANBY (GB) ch. 1857	WINDHOUND (GB)	br. 1847
				ALICE HAWTHORN (GB)	b. 1838
			ELLEN HORNE (GB) br. 1844	REDSHANK (GB)	b. 1833
				DELHI (GB)	blk. 1838
	LILY AGNES (GB) b. 1871	MACARONI (GB) b. 1860	SWEETMEAT (GB) dkb/br. 1842	GLADIATOR (GB)	ch. 1833
				LOLLYPOP (GB)	blk. 1836
			JOCOSE (GB) b. 1843	PANTALOON (GB)	ch. 1824
				BANTER (GB)	br. 1826
		POLLY AGNES (GB) br. 1865	THE CURE (GB) b. 1841	PHYSICIAN (GB)	b. 1829
				MORSEL (GB)	b. 1836
			MISS AGNES (GB) br. 1850	BIRDCATCHER (IRE)	ch. 1833
				AGNES (GB)	br. 1844
ANGELICA (GB) b. 1879	GALOPIN (GB) br. 1872	VEDETTE (GB) br. 1854	VOLTIGEUR (GB) br. 1847	VOLTAIRE (GB)	br. 1826
				MARTHA LYNN (GB)	br. 1837
			MRS RIDGWAY (GB) br. 1849	BIRDCATCHER (IRE)	ch. 1833
				NAN DARRELL (GB)	gr. 1844
		FLYING DUCH-ESS (GB) b. 1853	THE FLYING DUTCHMAN (GB) br. 1846	BAY MIDDLETON (GB)	b. 1833
				BARBELLE (GB)	b. 1836
			MEROPE (GB) b. 1841	VOLTAIRE (GB)	br. 1826
				JUNIPER MARE (GB)	br. 1817
	ST. ANGELA (GB) b. 1865	KING TOM (GB) b. 1851	HARKAWAY (IRE) ch. 1834	ECONOMIST (GB)	b. 1825
				FANNY DAWSON (IRE)	ch. 1823
			POCAHONTAS (GB) b. 1837	GLENCOE (GB)	ch. 1831
				MARPESSA (GB)	b. 1830
		ADELINE (GB) b. 1851	ION (GB) b. 1835	CAIN (GB)	b. 1822
				MARGARET (GB)	br. 1831
			LITTLE FAIRY (GB) ch. 1841	HORNSEA (GB)	ch. 1832
				LACERTA (GB)	b. 1816

'OUR' ARKLE

ARKLE (IRE) b. G, 1957. 35 Starts, 27 Wins, two 2nds, three 3rds, two fourths, unplaced once. Career Earnings: £95,198 Breeder: Mary Baker, Owner: Anne, Duchess Of Westminster.

ARKLE

Parents	Grandparents	Great-grandparents	Great-great-grandparents	Great-great-great-grandparents
ARCHIVE (GB) b. 1941	NEARCO (ITY) br. 1935 [BC]	PHAROS (GB) br. 1920 [I]	PHALARIS (GB) br. 1913 [B]	POLYMELUS (GB) b. 1902
				BROMUS (GB) b. 1905
			SCAPA FLOW (GB)* ch. 1914	CHAUCER (GB) br. 1900 [S]
				ANCHORA (GB) ch. 1905
		NOGARA (ITY)* b. 1928	HAVRESAC (FR) dkb/br. 1915 [I]	RABELAIS (GB) b. 1900 [P]
				HORS CON-COURS (FR) b. 1906
			CATNIP (IRE)* b. 1910	SPEARMINT (GB) b. 1903 [P]
				SIBOLA (USA) b. 1896
	BOOK LAW (GB)* b. 1924	BUCHAN (GB) b. 1916	SUNSTAR (GB) br. 1908 [S]	SUNDRIDGE (GB) ch. 1898
				DORIS (GB) br. 1898
			HAMOAZE (GB)* b. 1911	TORPOINT (GB) b. 1900
				MAID OF THE MIST (GB) b. 1906 *
		POPINGAOL (GB) br. 1913	DARK RONALD (IRE) blk/br. 1905 [P]	BAY RONALD (GB) b. 1893
				DARKIE (GB) blk. 1889
			POPINJAY (GB)* dkb/br. 1905	ST FRUSQUIN (GB) br. 1893
				CHELANDRY (GB) b. 1894 *
BRIGHT CHERRY (GB) ch. 1944	KNIGHT OF THE GARTER (GB) b. 1921	SON-IN-LAW (GB) dkb/br. 1911 [P]	DARK RONALD (IRE) blk/br. 1905 [P]	BAY RONALD (GB) b. 1893
				DARKIE (GB) blk. 1889
			MOTHER IN LAW (GB) b. 1906	MATCHMAKER (GB) b. 1892
				BE CANNIE (GB) ch. 1891
		CASTELLINE (GB) ch. 1908	CYLLENE (GB) ch. 1895	BONA VISTA (GB) ch. 1889
				ARCADIA (GB) ch. 1887
			CASSINE (FR) ch. 1898	XAINTRAILLES (FR) ch. 1882
				CROWFLOWER (GB) b. 1888
	GREENOGUE PRINCESS (GB) br. 1928	MY PRINCE (GB) b. 1911	MARCOVIL (GB) ch. 1903	MARCO (GB) ch. 1892
				LADY VILLIKINS (GB) ch. 1885
			SALVAICH (GB) b. 1896	ST SIMON (GB) br. 1881
				MUIRNINN (BEL) b. 1884
		CHERRY BRANCH (GB) ch. 1908	CERASUS (IRE) ch. 1897	CHERRY RIPE (GB) ch. 1884
				FELICITY (GB) b. 1890
			LADY PEACE (GB) b. 1903	GENERAL PEACE (IRE) br. 1894
				CLONEE (GB) ch. 1895

APPENDIX II:
WORLDWIDE
NAMING
PROTOCOL

WHAT'S IN A NAME?

Paul Palmer, Assistant Director and General Manager, and Director Horse Registry Department, Weatherbys GSB Ltd, explains:

'The name Arkle is protected, worldwide, against ever being used again for a thoroughbred. This despite the fact that jump racing is not particularly well served by the whole name protection process, as I will explain.

Every Racing Authority around the world has its own Rule Book. However, most will have been guided in setting their rules by The International Agreement on Racing, Breeding & Wagering, a best-practice document issued by the International Federation of Horseracing Authorities (IFHA). In terms of the length of time before a name becomes re-available, the International Agreement has this to say:

III Concerning names registered and not protected, the following criteria are provided as a guideline forming the basis upon which Authorities may establish a suitable period during which registered names will not be reused:

a) in the case of stallions, fifteen years after death or fifteen years after the last recorded year in which they covered mares or at thirty-five years of age (whichever is the soonest).

b) in the case of broodmares, ten years after their death or ten years after the last recorded year in which they were covered or produced a foal, or at twenty-five years of age.

c) in the case of all other horses, five years after their death, or at twenty years of age (whichever is the soonest). An exception may be made where the name of a horse which has been reported as dead and has not raced is sought for re-use by the same applicant.

'In addition to the above, IFHA have established an "International List of Protected Names", inclusion on which precludes a name from being re-used by any Recognised Racing Authority which signs up to the Naming element of the International Agreement. Qualification for protection is currently granted as follows:

1- Racehorses :

a) Automatic addition of the names of the winners of the following eleven most important international races for three year olds and upwards :

South America (2) : - Gran Premio Carlos Pellegrini, Grande Premio Brazil.

Asia (4) : - Melbourne Cup, Dubai World Cup, Hong Kong Cup, Japan Cup.

Europe (3) : - Prix de l'Arc de Triomphe, King George VI & Queen Elizabeth Stakes, Irish Champion Stakes.

USA (2) : - Breeders' Cup Classic, Breeders' Cup Turf.

b) Countries can propose to the IFHA Executive Council for approval, a maximum of three additional names per year of racehorses whose form justifies such a protection.

2. - Breeding stock :

Protection is given to :

Broodmares who have produced at least two Group 1 winners and one other Black Type winner.

Stallions who have produced at least fifteen individual Group 1 winners.

Within GB and Ireland (we are a joint Naming Authority), we protect additional names domestically, to prevent their re-use at least within our own area of jurisdiction. We routinely use this mechanism to protect the names of our Classic winners and those of celebrated National Hunt horses. No-one would wish to see another Desert Orchid, Kauto Star or Denman, or, of course, Arkle.'

APPENDIX III:
ARKLE'S RACING
RECORD

Date	Course	Race	Distance	Value	Weight (st, pb)	Starting price	Number of runners	Rider	Result
December 9, 1961	MULLINGAR, Co. Westmeath (closed 1967)	Lough Ennel Maiden NH Flat race	2miles 1 furlong	£133	11.4	5-1	17 ran	Mark Hely-Hutchinson	3rd
December 26	LEOPARDSTOWN, Co. Dublin	Greystones Maiden	2m	£202	10.11	5-1	10 ran	Mark Hely-Hutchinson	4th
January 20, 1962	NAVAN, Co. Meath	Bective Novice Hurdle	3m	£133	11.5	20-1	27 ran	L.McLoughlin	1st
March 10	NAAS, Co Kildare	Rathconnel Handicap Hurdle	2m	£202	11.2	2-1	10 ran	P.Taaffe	1st
April 14	BALDOYLE, Co Dublin (closed 1972)	Balbriggan H'cap Hurdle	2m	£387	10.1	6-1	18 ran	L.McLoughlin	0
April 14	FAIRYHOUSE, Co Meath	New H'cap Hurdle	2m	£742	10.5	8-1	9 ran	L. McLoughlin	4th
October 16	DUNDALK, Co Louth	Wee County H'cap Hurdle	2m 216 yards	£163	11.13	6-1	10 ran	P Taaffe	1st
October 24	GOWRAN PARK, Co Kilkenny		2m	£432	10.5	9-2	21 ran	P.Woods	1st
November 17	CHELTENHAM, Gloucestershire	Honeybourne Chase	2m 4f	£680	11.11	11-8	12 ran	P.Taaffe	1st

Date	Location	Race	Distance	Prize	Weight	Odds	Runners	Jockey	Position
February 23, 1963	LEOPARDSTOWN, Co Dublin	Milltown Chase	2m	£461.10s	12.11	1-2	15 ran	Pat Taaffe	1st
March 12	CHELTENHAM	Broadway Chase	3m and a few yards	£1,360	12.4	4-9	15 ran	Pat Taaffe	1st
April 15	FAIRYHOUSE	Power Gold Cup	2m 2f	£1,137	12.5	4-9	5 ran	Pat Taaffe	1st
May 1	PUNCHESTOWN, Co Kildare	John Jameson Cup	2m 4f	£852 15s	12.4	4-7	3 ran	Pat Taaffe	1st
October 9	NAVAN	Donoughmore Plate	1m 6f	£287	9.6	4-6	13 ran	T.P. Burns	1st
October 24	GOWRAN PARK	Carey's Cottage H'cap Chase	2m 4f	£519	11.13	4-7	10 ran	P.Taaffe	1st
November 30	NEWBURY, Berkshire	Hennessy Gold Cup	3m 2f 82 yards	£5020 10s	11.9	5-2	10 ran	P.Taaffe	3rd
December 26	LEOPARDSTOWN	Christmas H'cap Chase	3m	£846	12.0	4-7	6 ran	P.Taaffe	1st
January 30, 1964	GOWRAN PARK	Thyestes H'cap Chase	3m 170yds	£899 15s	12.0	4-6	9 ran	P.Taaffe	1st

February 15	Leopardstown	Leopardstown Chase	3m	£1,671	12.0	4-7fav	6 ran	P.Taaffe	1st
March 7	Cheltenham	Cheltenham Gold Cup	3m 2f	£8,004	12.0	7-4	4 ran	P.Taaffe	1st
March 30	Fairyhouse	Irish Grand National	3m 2f	£2,630	12.0	1-2fav	7 ran	P.Taaffe	1st
October 29	Gowran	Carey's Cottage H. Chase	2m 4f	£741	12.0	1-5fav	3 ran	P.Taaffe	1st
December 5	Newbury	Hennessy Gold Cup	3m 2f	£5,156	12.7	5-4fav	9 ran	P.Taaffe	1st
December 12	Cheltenham	Massey-Ferguson Cup	2m 5f	£3,989	12.10	8-11fav	7 ran	P.Taaffe	3rd
February 27 1965	Leopardstown	Leopardstown Chase	3m	£2,583	12.7	8-11fav	9 ran	P.Taaffe	1st
March 11	Cheltenham	Cheltenham Gold Cup	3m 2f	£7,986	12.0	30-100f	4 ran	P.Taaffe	1st
Apr 24	Sandown	Whitbread Gold Cup	3m 5f	£8,230	12.7	4-9fav	7 ran	P.Taaffe	1st

November 6	Sandown	Gallagher Gold Cup	3m	£5,165	12.7	4-9fav	7 ran	Pat Taaffe	1st
November 27	Newbury	Hennessy Gold Cup	3m 2f	£7,099	12.7	1-6fav	8 ran	Pat Taaffe	1st
December 27	Kempton	King George VI Chase	3m	£4,634	12.0	1-7fav	4 ran	Pat Taaffe	1st
March 1 1966	Leopardstown	Leopardstown Chase	3m	£2,475	12.7	1-5fav	4 ran	Pat Taaffe	1st
March 17	Cheltenham	Cheltenham Gold Cup	3m 2f	£7,764	12.0	1-10fav	5 ran	P. Taaffe	1st
November 26	Newbury	Hennessy Gold Cup	3m 2f	£5,713	12.7	4-6fav	6 ran	P. Taaffe	2nd
December 14	Ascot	S.G.B Chase	3m	£2,823	12.7	1-3fav	5 ran	P. Taaffe	1st
December 27	Kempton	King George VI Chase	3m	£3,689	12.7	2-9fav	7 ran	P. Taaffe	2nd

BIBLIOGRAPHY

Arkle, The Story of a Champion, Ivor Herbert, Pelham Books, 1966

Arkle, The Story of the World's Greatest Steeplechaser, Sean Magee, Highdown, 2005

Bend'Or, Duke of Westminster, George Ridley, Robin Clark Ltd, 1985

Dawn Run, Anne Holland, Arthur Barker, 1986

Drugs & Horses, Anne Holland, Compass Equestrian, 2000

Horses for Courses, Anne Holland, Mainstream Publishing, 2005

In the Blood, Irish Racing Dynasties, Anne Holland, The O'Brien Press, 2009

My Life & Arkle's, Pat Taaffe, Stanley Paul & Co Ltd, 1972

Nancy, The Story of Anne, Duchess of Westminster, 1915-2003, Robin Rhoderick-Jones, The Grosvenor Estate, 2008

Stan Mellor, A Thousand Winners, Introduction by John Francome (Publisher not recorded.)

Steeplechasing, A Celebration of 250 Years, Anne Holland, Little Brown 2001

Stride by Stride, the Illustrated Story of Horseracing, Anne Holland, Queen Anne Press, 1989

The Great Racehorses, Julian Wilson, Little Brown, 1987

The Irish Grand National, Stewart Peters, Stadia, 2007

T.P. Burns, A Racing Life, Guy St John Williams, Hillgate Publishing Ltd, 2006

First published 2013
by The O'Brien Press Ltd
12 Terenure Road East, Rathgar, Dublin 6, Ireland
Tel: +353 1 4923333; Fax: +353 1 4922777; Email: books@obrien.ie
Website: www.obrien.ie

ISBN: 978-1-84717-548-9

1 2 3 4 5 6 7 8 9 10
13 14 15 16 17

Printed and bound by ScandBook AB, Falun, Sweden 2013
The paper used in this book is produced using pulp from managed forests.

Picture credits:
Front cover: Injured wonder racehorse at Kempton Park Stables. (Photo by
Terrence Spencer//Time Life Pictures/Getty Images) 01/01/1967
Picture section 1: P 1 top left & right from *Bend'Or: Duke of Westminster* by
George Ridley (Robin Clark Ltd) (copyright unknown). P1 bottom; p3 bottom
left & right; p4 top left & bottom left; p5 bottom; p6 bottom; p7 top & bottom
from *Tom Dreaper and his Horses* by Bryony Fuller (Punchestown/Marlborough)
(copyright unknown). P2 top; p4 top right courtesy of Anne Holland. P2 bottom
image copyright © Alison Baker. P3 top image kindly supplied by Christina
Mercer. P5 top; p6 top copyright © Mirrorpix. P8 top copyright © Fox photos.
P8 bottom copyright © Sports & General.

Pic section 2: P1 top; p3 top; p4 top: from *Nancy: The Story of Anne, Duchess of
Westminster* by Robin Rhoderick-Jones (Granta); with thanks to The Grosvenor
Estate and the executors of Anne, Duchess of Westminster. P1 bottom *The Irish
Press*. P2 top and bottom copyright © Mirrorpix. P3 bottom image kindly sup-
plied by John Wilson. P4 bottom image kindly supplied by by Hellen Egan. P5
top image kindly supplied by The Irish National Stud. P 5 bottom copyright ©
Maxwell Photography. P6, 7 & p8 bottom courtesy of Anne Holland. P 8 top
image kindly supplied Lynsey Dreaper.